into the light

a memoir

ANNE WINTHROP CORDIN

Word Paint Publishing

Book & Cover Design: theartoftheword.com
Back Cover photography: Kathy Irving

ISBN 978-1732052444

Word Paint Publishing

For Leslie,
Who changed the trajectory
Of my life,
When she asked,
What are you waiting for?

Some say the past is best left in the past.
Some say we can and must learn from our mistakes.
Some say we're as sick as our secrets.
Some say we will not regret the past.
And I ask, *What do you say?*

1

I write to understand as much as to be understood. —Elie Wiesel

I dragged the diaper pail to the hallway and put it outside the front door for the weekly pickup.

The plastic container was heavy and the pre-rinse I gave the dirty diapers in the toilet did nothing to eliminate the acrid smell. Nor did the solid cake of air freshener fastened securely under the lid. It was a nasty, stinky job.

I quickly headed back inside the warm apartment.

I didn't notice that the heavy steel door wasn't shut tight. It had a safety feature which allowed it to close on its own, but on this frigid February morning the latch hadn't quite caught. The door was still slightly ajar.

Both the girls were still asleep, or they were at least quiet behind the closed door of their room. I could enjoy a few moments to myself before the clamor and duties of the day began. No immediate responsibilities, no one needing me for anything.

Kim would be two in two months; her baby sister would be one. Eleven months apart. Since finding out about my second unplanned pregnancy, I had been more lost and depressed than ever.

None of my friends even had children. And to tell the truth, the few friends I had made were now on the college track and I had lost touch with them. Their lives in no way resembled mine.

I had taken another direction.

And now I was a dreamer, always thinking about how things should have been. As time passed, I felt more and more powerless over my life. My life at nineteen.

My thoughts usually would begin: *if only*...then trail off to ideas and hopes that felt completely out of reach.

If only I didn't feel so trapped.

If only someone really understood me.

If only I had someone to talk to.

If only I hadn't gotten in trouble.

The girls were up and had finished breakfast, but we hadn't gotten much further with the day.

Life is but a dream.

My reverie splintered as the narcotics team came busting in—they didn't even have to knock.

The door that had been slightly ajar suddenly banged wide open, crashing back on its hinges, creating a chaos that shattered the morning's quiet. My husband, Billy, was at work, but our friend, George, was there. Billy would leave for work, the children playing with toys on the floor around us, the room a haze of smoke, the music always playing. George had slept over again, passed out on the couch after we sat up late talking. He was always there, hanging out, drinking, and getting high with us. George had a different way of looking at things and conversation with him was probing, challenging, and I started to feel like I was waking up when he came around. I sat like a pupil at the foot of a prophet.

As they searched our apartment, throwing our things around, turning the sofa cushions over, pulling sheets off the beds, ripping even the children's clothes in the closets from their shelves and hangers, I was doing everything I could to keep the girls calm and hide the truth.

–Mommy didn't do anything wrong.

–No, no, now don't cry, everything is going to be okay.

Tears streaked my face when a female officer took them away.

–I'll keep them safe while this gets sorted out, she said to no one in particular.

With the neighbors watching, I was loaded, handcuffed, into an unmarked police car.

Too many hippies coming in and out, there's got to be something going on in there. They probably have drugs in there. They might even be dealing out of the apartment. We can't have this going on here; we're decent people after all.

Cars in the parking lot that didn't belong to the residents had raised suspicion and the gossip grew. Some nosy neighbor had made the phone call, expressing concern.

A thorough search of the apartment by the narcotics team came up with less than a nickel bag of pot, some rolling papers, and a little onyx pipe we used for hash.

They had actually come at a good time, considering. There wasn't any hash and we normally had a lot more pot stashed here and there.

Thanks to that anonymous tip, we had been under surveillance for the last six months.

It reinforced everything I felt about society, straight people, people over thirty and people who didn't have anything better to do than spy on us.

Why couldn't they just mind their own damn business?

Was I paranoid? Maybe. Probably.

I distrusted people I didn't know. I had plenty of

contempt for them as well. Quick to judge, I felt somehow that I was unique and should play by different rules—my rules—which changed on a whim and by the situation.

That was part of the problem.

There was no regularity or routine in anything I did, nothing I could count on, and it made me very insecure. I constantly felt like I was missing something—that other people somehow knew things I hadn't learned, and it didn't feel fair. My insides were a mass of confusion and anxiety. Deep under that lay fear.

*

The original felony charge was reduced to possession—a misdemeanor.

There weren't any other female inmates in that county jail while I was there. Not accustomed to my own company, certainly not without any drugs or alcohol to take the edge off my feelings, loneliness and worry set in.

I couldn't stop worrying about what was happening to my girls, what was going to happen.

In the meantime, I found out from my lawyer they had been placed in foster homes for their own safety.

This made me even more anxious.

Their safety was a concept I had never considered. It seemed completely insane. How could they not be safe if they were with me? I was their mother.

I soon discovered the courts were not in a big hurry to give me my children back.

My drinking and drug use had gotten me into many situations I never planned on. It had taken me places I didn't want to be. But now my girls were in foster homes with strangers. This was the worst by far.

As the time wore on, I began to think that maybe they weren't safe with me. When I started drinking, I couldn't predict the consequences; I never knew what might happen.

*

They took my leather belt so that I wouldn't hang myself or slit my wrists with the metal buckle.

My birth control pills had been taken away too and after a couple of days in jail, I noticed spotting. Then my period came. The guard outfitted me unsympathetically with an old-fashioned, oversized sanitary pad and belt.

In that cage, I felt total humiliation all the time. There was no door to shut for privacy and nowhere to hide behind the bars from the eyes of the people who passed by each day.

I couldn't believe this was how I was being treated.

The narcs kept asking me the same questions over and over, hoping I would mess up with different answers—give something away about George or Billy or the source of the drugs—but that didn't happen.

The phone connection from the county jail was bad but I filled my parents in on what had happened. I kept the emotion out of my voice. I didn't ask for help or advice of any kind. I thought I should be able to figure this out on my own.

Then I told them about the girls and the foster homes. I didn't think how they must have really taken this news. I didn't want to think about what they must have been feeling.

After we hung up, I imagined how the conversation went between my parents. There was probably some mention of God.

—We're going to have to trust God with this one, my

father might have said.

He would have tried to reassure my mother, but they both knew there wasn't a damn thing they could do.

Once again, I was in a mess, and their hearts were suffering collateral damage. I never for a moment, not one moment, considered how my actions were affecting my parents.

*

I spent a week in that small cell in the Fairfax County jail before I was released and the charges dropped. I was free on condition of good behavior for a year.

My lawyer told me that my husband couldn't be located. Billy had taken off when he heard what happened—he wasn't going to be around to risk getting busted. Even so, I couldn't believe that he would just disappear. The police considered George to be the ring leader, but they couldn't find much to pin on him either.

And so I went home. George came along too.

George had grown up in the system and his stories of foster homes made my heart ache. I couldn't just leave the girls there indefinitely. I just didn't know what to do, but I needed to do something soon.

George asked in no uncertain terms whether I thought I was capable of caring for them.

—Are you going to stop getting high?

—Are you going to stop drinking?

—How much do you think you can really change?

The seeds of doubt grew and sprouted and spread like cancer.

I wasn't a good enough mother.

Someone else could do it better.

The final decision didn't happen immediately.

It was over the course of several long nights and days, fueled by pot and alcohol that my thinking degraded. The stoned conversations with George, the grim details of his boyhood sealed my children's fate.

I decided that letting them be adopted *would* be the best thing I could do for them.

I didn't seek any counsel when making this monumental decision. I focused only on how everyone could have a new and better life if I let them go.

I thought we could *all* start over.

My husband and I formally separated; our marriage ending before it had even begun.

So many details are lost in the fog of time.

Here's what I do remember with great clarity. My chance at motherhood had failed which meant I was a dismal failure as a human being.

The day came and as I signed the final papers in front of the judge, he spoke from his high bench in a voice full of contempt.

–I've never seen anyone like you before.

–Even animals don't desert their young.

His disgust was obvious.

I hated him. I forced back the tears so that no one would see how misunderstood I felt.

Why didn't I fight for my daughters?

Why didn't anyone fight for them?

Why did I allow things to unfold as they did?

How had things gone so out of control?

These questions became my nightmares.

*

In the following weeks, I would drink and call the social worker and tell her how I had made a terrible mistake. I cried with the phone pressed hard against my temple, and she would tell me that it was too late and that I should get on with my life.

I tried desperately to keep her on the line, but she had nothing more to add.

She never told me exactly how to get on with my life and no amount of wine or pot provided the answer.

Remorse. Guilt. Shame. I felt them all, even if I couldn't put a name to those feelings at the time.

How could you?

How could you abandon your children?

You ARE worse than an animal.

How could you?

The biggest decision of my life had been made under the influence of alcohol and drugs.

*

Years later, while researching these events, I had a phone conversation with a social worker who read the court's adoption proceeding transcript to me. I was searching for insight into my frame of mind at the time; to better understand how I could have come up with my decision.

I was described as alert, articulate and seeming to be in possession of her right mind.

I looked the judge square in the eye and stated my wishes.

I asked for a copy of the transcript and was denied. Overworked, desks piled with cases like mine, the social worker could only do so much.

With kindness, she too said I needed to move on.

Would any more detail really help me understand my exact state of mind, help me forgive myself for my actions? What happened, happened, and I would never be able to change that.

I had to find a way to move forward and do as the social worker urged.

Forget about the past.

All this awareness about events when I was nineteen has been very slow to come by.

With my thinking clouded and distorted by alcohol and drugs, I had made a monumental life-changing decision for my daughters.

Even so, I know today I made the best decision I could at the time.

If I had known better, I might have done better.

Wanting something better for them than I could give; a family where they were wanted from the beginning, where the children's needs came first; this was my heart's wish for them.

Years of pain and addiction were to follow that my daughters were spared living through.

I told myself I was a horrible mother and didn't deserve them anyway.

They were gone.

I had nothing left to lose.

2

Not knowing anything is the sweetest life. —Sophocles

I didn't start out like that.

I had been a happy kid, full of confidence and curiosity. With lots of friends, I never felt I was different than anyone else. In fact, I felt good about myself, confident and smart, happy and strong.

Knowing I had been adopted as an infant didn't play on my mind—I never thought about my birth mother or her circumstances—and I pretty much skipped through my early childhood, secure in being me.

My parents had been married almost ten years. They married the day after my father graduated from the Naval Academy.

After a couple of miscarriages and disappointment took hold, a family doctor and friend who practiced in New Hampshire, suggested adoption. He said he sometimes helped arrange private adoptions for his patients.

It gave my parents hope.

Maybe they *would* have a baby after all.

My mother was in a still-life class at the Art Association in Newport, Rhode Island, concentrating on painting a chianti bottle and a duck decoy when they got the phone call that changed everything. A baby had been born and the mother wasn't going to keep her. Were they interested?

Yes, they were. And so the chosen baby story that I was to know by heart was also born.

My parents rushed to purchase a layette, packed the car, and headed north to meet the baby girl they had thought of naming Victoria.

Once they saw me, they decided I looked more like an Anne. My middle name was hefty for a baby—Winthrop—after John Winthrop, the first governor of Massachusetts, a distant relative.

Straight from the hospital at five days old to the doctor's house where my parents got a crash course in *Baby 101* before bringing me home to Newport.

Then came a Navy transfer to Norfolk, and while they were thinking of nothing but me and my dad's new job, Mummy found out she was pregnant. Without even trying this time, my sister Marjorie was born when I was two and a half. And so we were four.

Ten years of normal.

No red flags to predict the disaster that was to come.

It all came to a screeching halt when Daddy got transferred to France.

I had just finished fifth grade and felt expectantly free. At first the move seemed so exciting; we would be having a real adventure.

Our transatlantic passage on an ocean liner was loads of fun. We played Bingo, ate shrimp cocktail, and dressed up each night for dinner. I raced around the decks with kids I never would see again and got a taste of what I thought real life was all about.

We settled into our apartment in St Germaine-en-Laye, a suburb about twelve miles west of Paris. It was the birthplace of Louis XIV which meant nothing to me.

Our neighbors had rabbits and we thought it sweet until we learned they were being raised for food. Knowing how they would meet their end took the fun out of looking in and petting them.

School was starting soon but we weren't going to the American School in Paris, where most of the US kids went.

L'Institute of Notre Dame was a convent school that our mother thought would be the best and fastest way for us to learn the language. It was all girls, all French, and we were the only English-speaking students there.

I should have started worrying when we went uniform shopping; the clothes were all so heavy and dark. The only redeeming item was a snappy little beret which I thought made me look very French. I hoped looking the part might help me fit in. There was a lot to get used to. Way too much, I thought to myself.

Instead of going into sixth grade, I was now in the fourth. Instead of being with girls who were ten years old like me, I was with girls who were eight.

Because she doesn't speak French was the reasoning they gave my parents.

My classmates were tiny, mean and Catholic. Everything they said to me was referenced by the fact that I was Protestant. I had never thought of my religion as something that anyone would hold against me, but now it seemed to be a real shortcoming and I didn't know why. None of it made sense; I was Episcopalian and had just been confirmed in a starched white dress and veil in a regally beautiful ceremony at the American Church in Paris on the Quai D'Orsey.

They did everything they could to make me feel like the big, old, American Protestant girl I was. There was nothing cool about being American in this school.

Shunned and teased by my classmates, understanding nothing of what was going on in class, I started having feelings I had never experienced before.

The social rejection I felt gave rise to the thought that there was something the matter with me.

For the first time I wondered, *Why don't they like me? What is wrong with me?*

Understanding the language around me was a basic I had taken for granted, and I sat dazed and sleepy through hours of classes. I was constantly being told to sit up and wake up.

—*Tenez-vous droit!*

—*Reveillez-vous!*

Handwriting skill was highly regarded, and I learned to slant my letters in that particular French schoolgirl way the nuns insisted on. Here at least was one thing I could do well and I ignored my cramping fingers as I copied page after page with the thin violet ink from the inkwell built into the small desk.

I learned to memorize lines for recitation of history and long passages of literature. Recitation was valued more than discussion, so I practiced my French at home learning to speak without an American accent. I had to get rid of all traces of the American girl that I was.

So awkwardly out of place, so lonely, and so very different from my classmates—the feelings were very confusing.

I knew I would never belong.

And I knew that all my efforts didn't make any difference to them.

When our mother dropped us off in the cobblestoned courtyard of the school entry, Marjorie and I would hold onto the door handles of the car for as long as we could as she slowly drove off.

After the long and tedious day, we couldn't wait for *le gouter*, the tea that marked the end of the school day at 4:30. However sweet the chocolate croissants or *pain d'epices*, a sort of gingerbread, it didn't take away the sour taste of being there.

In the hallway leading to the bathrooms, at the landing of a wide and sweeping staircase, a stooped over and ancient nun sat on a three-legged stool by a stack of newspapers. She tore them into appropriate bottom-wiping-sized strips which were dropped into a basket for us. You weren't encouraged to take more than one.

What, there wasn't any toilet paper?

It wasn't long before we started bringing little packets of Kleenex with us to school.

The school was awful, and our complaints were constant, but within three months we understood what we were hearing and conversational French came soon after.

Mummy was delighted; her girls were bilingual.

—It hasn't been *that* bad has it, girls?

We had no choice but to agree with her.

*

Several months later we were at a large and festive Baptism party. My mother had hired a housekeeper, someone to go to the market and speak French with. Renee and my mother became quite good friends and she had asked my parents to be godparents to her baby, Laurence. The baptism itself had been rather unremarkable, long and undecipherable in Latin, held in a dark and musty church. The smell of incense was heavy and pigeons flew high into the rafters. Afterwards we gathered in a high-ceiling hall rented for the event and were seated at long banquet tables. Mounds of pink and white candy-coated almonds were scattered around the place settings and wine was being poured. Everyone was getting served; adults and children alike. We were in France, after all.

That first taste did it for me.

It felt like heaven.

My self-conscious awkwardness dissolved with each sip. Everything in that old hall sparkled, from the glasses to the glittery jewelry the women wore, to their gold teeth peeking through their lips as they spoke.

I spoke French, I laughed, and I knew I had found the answer to my problems.

The band began to play, and someone asked me to dance. Being whirled around that tiny dance floor I felt like I was in a storybook tale or on a stage of a fanciful, dreamy musical. I had at last found what made me fit in in France and it wasn't the language. It was the glass of wine. I no longer had the uncomfortable feeling of being so strange, so foreign, so different from everyone around me. It leveled us all, creating a camaraderie strengthened by each toast and raise of the glass.

I was a sitting duck for my first experience with alcohol. I was vulnerable and didn't know it. It made all my fear, insecurities and worries fly out the door and a shining, bright promise that everything was fine replaced it.

It was better than fine.

I loved what alcohol did for me. It transported me to another place. A place of belonging.

I never put my hand over the top of the glass to signify I'd had enough; there was no stopping once I started.

Why would I want to stop anyway? It was the first drink

that activated my cravings for alcohol.

This phenomenon can be explained through an understanding of the neurotransmitter dopamine.

Dopamine is released in limbic areas of the brain when a drug is taken and it doesn't differentiate between legal or illegal drugs. Food and sex are also related to increases in dopamine but in the non-addict the level drops after the appetite is sated. Not so with drugs; the dopamine level remains high as the addict repeats the reinforcing behavior and becomes conditioned to the drug, creating a need to use more and more.

The dopamine release reinforces the drug use as the drug dose that equaled happiness no longer gives the same result. Neurons are reactivated when the expectations aren't met and the cravings increase.

More drugs for more happiness.

The vulnerable individual has lost control and is left with only the urge to keep taking the substance in increasing amounts dictated by a dopamine system that has been hijacked. In recovery, it's explained as the phenomena of craving.

Addiction is thought to be 50% genetically determined and exposure to drugs at an early age will increase the chances of addiction.

The adolescent brain has a neural plasticity and the adaptive processes can happen all the more easily.

Two characteristics of addiction were present: a stress surfeit disorder and a self-regulation disorder.

In other words, I was fucked from the very start.

I didn't want to stop drinking that wine; I loved the

transforming effect alcohol had.

I had found a solution and I loved how it made me feel. I felt connected to everyone around me.

The paradox was, that at the end of my drinking fifteen years later, I felt completely and totally isolated and alone. How had this happened to me?

3

We live in a fantasy world, a world of illusion. The great task in life is to find reality. –Iris Murdoch

We ended up leaving the French school midyear the second year—Mummy got *Hepatitis A* and couldn't drive us anymore. She was flat out in bed for a couple of months after my sister noticed her eyes were yellow instead of white. Something was very wrong.

She had eaten some bad *mussels meuniere*, or maybe it was oysters on the half shell on a trip to Deauville. We felt sorry for her, but for us it was a stroke of luck. We had to get an injection of immunoglobulin so that we wouldn't get sick too, but we didn't care. It was a small price to pay for getting out of the school we both hated.

Now we were at the American School in Paris. It was a typical big public school with such large class sizes that you could almost go unnoticed. Changing classrooms, lockers, cafeteria pecking order, were all new to me. Once again, feelings of being defenseless rushed me and fitting in became my daily challenge.

Who do I make friends with?
How do I get them to like me?
Am I wearing the right clothes?
Am I saying the right things?
Am I okay?

Had I just been myself, and not been so worried about people liking me, my schooldays might have gone differently.

Instead I went to the PX and brought home a stack of romance and movie star magazines. I was obsessed with American culture and lived in a fantasy through the stories and magazine pictures. I made scrapbooks filled with Sandra Dee, Annette, and Troy Donahue.

Maybe now I can figure out how to be.

Brenda Lee had come out with *I'm Sorry* and it hit number one on the US charts. I stole it from a local record store for no reason at all. I didn't think about the consequences, about what my parents might say.

My impulsivity sprung out from me that afternoon, untamed and uncontrollable. I wanted excitement and when I ran from the store, my heart pounding, I got a rush that was new.

Risk-taking made me feel alive and high. It covered up other feelings I didn't like; being an outsider, misunderstood and unloved.

*

We had an English cousin, Marjorie, who had a country cottage and we would fly to Heathrow and take the train to Twyford to visit her.

Old roses in silver vases were in every wallpapered room of the little house and their scent filled the space. It left an impression of an old-fashioned time of elegance and whispered conversations.

Every afternoon we had English High Tea with scones, clotted cream and fresh, ripe strawberries from the kitchen garden.

Back in London, we stayed at Brown's Hotel and went on

long rambles through the museums, the gardens and my favorite place, Piccadilly Circus.

The excited energy was such a strong contrast from Cousin Marjorie's lovely but staid and quiet home, and it thrilled me just to be there.

Books had now become my surest escape and the book department at Harrod's was always a stop where I lingered through the shelves until my parents called me away.

I could spend hours in a good bookstore getting lost in the possibilities of adventure and belonging the pages of my favorite books held. Never able to settle on just one, I left with a parcel of anticipated pleasure in print.

My first period came on a visit to London.

I had been begging my mother for months to let me wear stockings. I had a friend in my class who wore them, and I wanted to be like her.

Of course, she thought Kathy was growing up too fast, but I thought she just wanted to keep me a little girl as long as she could. She had said I would have to wait until I started my period.

That night I wasn't a little girl anymore and when we went down to the elegant hotel dining room, I had on a new garter belt with stockings. I was also wearing a sanitary belt and a fat puffy pad.

Daddy raised his glass.

–Congratulations, Annie. I understand you've become a young woman.

I couldn't have been any more embarrassed, sure that his voice had carried to every other diner in the restaurant. I turned beet red, as red as the blood I wanted to deny.

He was proud, and I wanted to die.

How could my mother have betrayed me like that? Why

had I even told her? I was sure this was something not to be talked about. It was something that should be referred to only with code words.

I've got my friend this week. I've got the curse. I'm cursed.

I stuffed down the shame and just kept glancing down at the silky stockings I had earned the right to wear. I sipped on my cherry-stained Shirley Temple. Now I could be like the other girls.

*

After less than a full year at the American School in Paris, my dad was transferred again. He was going to be the captain of the flagship of the Sixth Fleet, and the home port was Villefranche—a deep-water harbor and picturesque town filled with buildings that dated back to the twelfth and thirteenth century.

The USS *Springfield* had fought in the Pacific during WWII and was later converted to a guided-missile cruiser. The change of command took place in Athens in April, which was all very exciting, and then the ship came home. Images of marble and limestone ruins under a hot, blue sky devoid of clouds, were the memories that stayed with me.

The bay of Villefranche has Nice on one side and Cap Ferrat on the other, in the center of the famed Cote D'Azur on the Mediterranean Coast.

We were going to live on the French Riviera and I conjured up images of romance and excitement.

Our house in St Jean Cap Ferrat was surrounded by a high wall which was typical in our neighborhood. Our garden was filled with orange and fig trees and the lavender which grew in wild abundance in the mild Mediterranean climate.

My bedroom was on the first floor, which made sneaking

out much easier. I had made friends with a group of older kids and they convinced me to join them for some fun. It didn't take much, I wanted some excitement and that adrenaline rush.

The British came to town to make a movie, and my mother became very involved in that. She spent weeks on the set, watching the filming, meeting the actors, and generally being unavailable to us. She told us they needed her to run their lines with.

She had tea in Monaco with Princess Grace; the heavily embossed invitation had been hand-delivered. Glamor, glittering lights, and a constant stream of sophisticated parties to attend on the arm of my father were all hers now.

Whenever the ship left port, she followed.

I thought I didn't care.

I thought I didn't need her.

I thought she was too busy for me.

It was obvious she was having the best time of her life.

*

My father stayed many nights aboard ship. He said the house was damp and full of mold which kicked up his asthma. There were the stray cats too that wheedled their way inside the house. He was happier on his ship. On rare special occasions, we stayed at a hotel when the ship was in port and we could be together as a family again.

Mummy must have been lonely at times, with just us girls in the house. She would sit by the window with a drink and a book, smoking her unfiltered Pall Malls. I had been snitching those cigarettes from her on a regular basis, thinking that she didn't notice.

One night she said, —If you want to smoke, for God's sake, don't pinch them. Here, have one with me.

I felt very grown up at that point.

I was thirteen going on twenty.

*

My friends and I rented pedalos from the beach and we went out to see the ship, waving to the sailors working on deck as we pedaled around all six hundred and ten feet of her.

Tanned and bikinied, laughing at private jokes, we were having fun.

I felt safe and bold and afraid all at the same time.

I hoped that Daddy wouldn't peer down and spot me though; I knew that could mean trouble. The last thing my father needed was to worry about me.

We went to an English school called the Anglo-American Children's Club in nearby Beaulieu-sur-Mer. Unlike the American School in Paris, the class size was small, and the wonderful teachers knew us all by name.

Able to combine art with science got me participating and feeling that school wasn't so dreadful after all. I actually wanted to do the work.

Individual attention was what I needed, and in this small school I was finally getting it. There were one or two teachers who were sensitive, and I thrived for the short time I was there.

I did a report on the *eye* accompanied by precise pencil drawings. I created pen and ink drawings of branches and flowers that I finished with soft watercolor washes. Such projects absorbed me totally, allowing me to create without thought. No stress of emotion, no consequences of my chaotic nocturne escapades.

I started to feel inspired.

It didn't last.

*

So needy for attention; experimenting with alcohol, smoking and my nighttime excursions with the twilight crowd contrasted sharply with the good girl persona I had in school. No one suspected that I was living a double life.

I hurried past the groups of Algerians who camped near the path to the sea.

Algeria had just gained independence from France, but there was still a palpable tension I didn't understand.

Political rights that had been denied, substandard housing and few opportunities to rise above poverty levels kept many Algerians grumbling and marginalized.

I was in another world, living a privileged life, and in that summer of 1962, I cared more about Bridgette Bardot, Bob Dylan's first album and the first James Bond movie, *Dr. No.*

I was a teenager.

I would meet friends and drink for hours and somehow stumble back home, unlatch the heavy gate just enough to slip through, and crawl into bed unnoticed.

Later that summer, I got friendly with a sailor and he would drive us through winding mountain roads out by the airport where we would park and drink.

I would smoke and stare at blue lights flickering in the distance as he explored parts of me that should have remained uncharted for many more years. I imagined myself part of a movie scene, and like a movie, it would soon be over. I disassociated without knowing what I was doing.

I didn't dare say no. After all, he was nice enough to give me cigarettes and drinks and pick me up for exhilarating nights out.

I wasn't positive about it, but I didn't think I was doing anything that wrong.

Boundaries are what you learn to show respect for yourself and others. It wasn't something I had ever been taught. Maybe other people had natural boundaries, but I didn't. I thought I owed him for the attention he gave me.

*

Daytime had me on the beach by ten o'clock and the hours would pass sunbathing and going in and out of the water.

The Plage de Passable was in a quiet cove, very safe and within a short distance from our house. Mummy would drive us there and I would take off as soon as I spotted my friends. Hanging out all day with my mother and Marjorie was the last thing I wanted to do now that school was out.

It was much nicer to be with my friends. I wanted to fall asleep and let the sun beat down on me. We would eat ice cream and drink sweet orange soda, looking at boys while we smoked.

One of the boys from my new group of friends was the son of a famous British actor—yet another one who got closer than I should have let him. He lived in a big pink house that had once been owned by Charlie Chaplin, with steps to the sea. The path that led out to the spit of land reminded me of the Cliff Walk in Newport, populated with homes of the rich and famous.

I didn't seem to have any limits around my body; I didn't

think anything was a big deal. What was all the fuss about? The stories in romance magazines were my main source of information about relationships and I longed for connection and a feeling of being wanted. I would do anything to get that feeling.

Another transfer came for Daddy, this time as Chief of Staff for the Commander Cruiser-Destroyer Force which brought us back to the States and Newport in March of 1963.

After an agonizing time, I finished eighth grade and I shook that school loose like a dog coming out of the ocean. Four years had passed but I was now light years away from those same kids. Having lived in ways no one could relate to, I felt even more cut off and isolated. I had nothing in common with any of them. I had been living life largely unsupervised and doing as I pleased. All my classmates seemed so very young to me.

Misplaced and lost.

Unreachable and sulky.

Secretive and uncommunicative.

That's when my parents came up with the plan to send me to boarding school.

4

I had nothing to offer anybody except my own confusion.

—Jack Kerouac

Another set of orders came for Daddy; he was headed to DC for an important job at the Pentagon.

My parents needed to know I was safe so they wouldn't have to constantly worry about me.

They were trying to get some order in my life—order they hadn't been able to impose.

They felt boarding school was the best option.

If I had been a boy, they would have sent me to military school.

I felt like I was being shipped off. Like they were trying to get rid of me.

All the new clothes and shoes from Lord & Taylor and Pappagallos didn't make me feel any better. I went off with suitcases stuffed full of plaids, knee socks and Peter Pan collars. I wanted to look like everyone else. I was furious they were doing this to me. I hadn't had any say in the matter and it made me mad. They just wouldn't listen.

September found me unpacking and feeling frightened by the experience of being away from home. Concord, Massachusetts, is a small town noted in history as the site of the first battle in the Revolutionary War. I wasn't much interested in history.

Everyone at the school seemed to know each other

already. Once again, I felt sensitive and left out. Ninth grade and I was immediately overwhelmed by my classmates' intensity and competitiveness.

My roommate was from Texas and had brought her electric guitar and her enthusiasm for life. She was loud as hell and her brassiness and wide smile had everyone around her laughing. She was athletic and made friends quickly. I took note of this as I compared myself to her. I didn't know any team sports, hadn't learned tennis, and felt shy and awkward as I huddled with all those bare red legs in New England fall afternoons. I was usually the last one chosen for teams. I didn't make friends quickly.

There were a few classes I was interested in—literature and art—where I actually did well.

I loved to read, write and draw. I loved my art class and learned about the Old Masters and my favorites, the Impressionists. Renoir paintings of demure pink-faced girls with flowing tresses sitting in sunny flower-filled gardens transported me to where I could smell lavender and hear the buzz of bees. This idyllic countryside gathering seemed so lush and pretty and filled my imagination with happy times and friends I didn't have and somehow filled my hungry heart. The heavy-lidded women that Modigliani painted looked how I felt inside. I didn't know how to express any of this longing.

Anyway, who could I talk to about this?

Soon after school started, I began hanging out with a boy I met in the little market his father owned—an historic building converted to a grocery store by an enterprising Norwegian ancestor at the end of the nineteenth century.

He was a townie, but I didn't care.

He could get beer. He became my beer contact and

boyfriend. Interchangeable.

My risk-taking increased in proportion to my anxiety and sense of apartness from most of my classmates.

Pushing the pedals hard on my new bike, I made my way through town, turning northeast by the Monument Square flagpole and the Colonial Inn. I pushed on up the hill to Sleepy Hollow Cemetery.

Hidden among the trees, we would meet at Authors Ridge.

I was among the graves of authors I admired; Louisa May Alcott, Hawthorne, and Thoreau, but I was oblivious to the history as I chugged my beer and forgot about all the classes and kids I hated. I didn't have anything in common with any of them.

Not belonging was a feeling I was getting too used to.

There was one smart and athletic girl whose long-muscled legs filled me with envy. She was my first crush. We shared snacks in her room and I felt I could be myself around her.

Soon I was thinking how she had it made.

I watched her on the hockey field and started begrudging how simple everything seemed for her.

I took to blaming others for my unhappiness.

This was normally a long mental tirade of how things weren't fair, and people were mean and didn't care about me anyway.

I wouldn't uncover my distorted perceptions for years.

All the other girls seemed to have an idea of what they might like to do with their lives; at the very least they all had something they were passionate about, whether it was racing around the hockey field or playing some instrument or learning Shakespeare to be in a play.

My parents found a tutor for me in Concord, a lovely lady

who made tea and tried hard to teach me some good study habits to keep me from falling behind.

Twice a week, back and forth in a yellow cab. In the end, I just didn't care; it didn't seem important enough to me to change my approach and buckle down to work. I didn't use any of the tools developed just for kids like me.

*

John F. Kennedy was assassinated on November 22 and our school came to a grinding halt. Classes were sparsely attended, and teachers kept losing their train of thought. We were all in a daze and half the student body went home to their families. The rest of us sat and watched TV for hours on the day JFK was buried. After that, nothing seemed like it could be counted on anymore.

To have the entire country in mourning saddened and confused me.

Who was going to fix it?

I felt an enormous sense of powerlessness and with no grief counseling, no one trained to talk with us, and no explanation for the sense of doom I carried in such an unpredictable world.

After Thanksgiving and back at school, I thought of Caroline and John-John with no daddy and I couldn't concentrate on anything.

I drank every chance I got and found that getting numb helped. I was too sensitive. I told myself that I needed to toughen up.

The year droned on and my disinterest was palpable.

I sat through algebra classes that made my eyelids go heavy and before long there was no catching up.

That meant summer school at St Albans in Washington, where my parents now lived.

I was losing ground academically.
I didn't care.
I just wanted to sleep.
I made promises I couldn't keep.

5

If you don't know where you are going any road can take you there.
—Lewis Carroll

During the summer between ninth and tenth grade, I started hanging out with a boy whose sister I had been friends with. Somehow, I ended up spending the night at his house. My parents were obviously off in their own world otherwise they might not have thought it appropriate that I sleep over at a boy's house at my age.

There had never been any discussions of sex in my family and I hadn't had the conversation with anyone.

I thought that experience was the best teacher; that's how I had learned everything so far.

With little else to go by, the stories in the romance magazines had had a big impact on me.

This boy had places we could go and be alone. Bunk beds in his room. A little sailboat at the dock down the street. A pup tent behind his house nestled in a grove of trees.

We had been sneak drinking all afternoon. There was always sneak drinking going on in people's homes. We drank in elaborately decked out rec rooms with parents who believed it would be okay because they were around.

We'd rather have them here having a party then out somewhere they might get in trouble.

They sat upstairs reading a Book of the Month Club pick

with a sweaty Old-Fashioned on the side table next to them. Every now and again, they would come to the top of the basement stairs and call down.

—Is everyone having fun down there?

—Sure, mom.

We would all be quiet until the door shut again and then go back to drinking and games of *Spin the Bottle* and *Post Office*. There was always a stack of 45's that we'd dance to, the slow ones leading to make-out sessions in the back of the closet among the off-season clothes.

We'd emerge hot and sweaty challenging eye contact with our friends.

*

It happened in the pup tent.

I looked up at the light filtering through the green fabric, at the mosquitos clinging to the tent walls. I felt the hard ground under me and wondered what I had missed.

So, this was it?

The big *IT*.

It had been awkward, all the fumbling, then painful in a jabbed flash. All the pushing made my breath ragged and my elbows hurt digging into the tent floor.

I wondered when my body would quiver and my skin would feel electric.

I had been reading countless accounts of this experience in *True Confessions*.

Somehow my experience wasn't anything like what I had read. Where were the soft words, the brush of lips against my neck, and the tender circle of arms?

This was a serious disappointment.

Clearly not the world changing experience I had hoped

for. It had been easier to say yes than say no, especially after a couple of drinks.

We lay there afterwards, but not for long; we wanted to have a smoke and had to go down to the little sailboat to do that.

I pulled up my shorts and panties which had been pushed down around my ankles and smoothed my clothes. I pushed open the flap door of the tent and stepped into the brilliant sunlight of that late July afternoon. He had never declared love or any affection; he just wanted to *do it*.

I hadn't thought too much about the consequences.

I really couldn't think of any reason not to go all the way.

I really hadn't thought too much at all.

I had hoped it might change me into another person; a person who knew something important.

And then summer vacation was over, and it was time to go back to school.

6

Life is made up of marble and mud. –Nathaniel Hawthorne

Two weeks into tenth grade, I got caught smoking on the roof of my dorm.

I had climbed out the window and thought I was hidden in the eaves of the old house.

Someone had spotted me and turned me in. I was suspended for a week and my father flew up to Boston. He rented a car and drove me back to DC.

He gave me the silent treatment for hours, and then talked nonstop, even when I pretended to be asleep with my face pressed against the window.

His words droned on and I tried not to hear the disappointment and frustration in his voice.

If only I could have explained to him how scared and lonely I felt.

What my head told me was this: Everyone at school seems to know how to do everything. I don't.

They were born wearing tennis whites and played hockey while I played jacks.

They told me about their skiing vacations. I'd never even been on skis.

How can I compete with these girls, everything comes so easily for them?

I don't know how I can do the work that this school expects of me—

I'm so far behind everyone else.

Everyone is taking it so seriously, they've been talking about college since last year.

All the demands on me are frightening.

I'm afraid that even if I try as hard as I can I can't catch up.

I was in France when they learned sentence structure and I sit mystified in English.

I don't even know how to think about my life. I don't know what to consider or even how to begin. I see only black or white with nothing in between.

Who can show me the way?

Who can help me?

I'm just too afraid to ask since I'm sure I'm the only one who feels this way. I don't know anything about anything.

Suspension ended after a week with no privileges and I returned to school, vowing to be better, to be good, to follow the rules, to not get in trouble.

It didn't last.

I was failing geometry before the leaves dropped in crumbling piles to the ground. It was as if a course had been set and no amount of fidgeting with the steering could right the way.

The constant comparing myself to my classmates had me always coming up short, but I didn't have a clue how to fix myself.

Even with the best intentions, I just couldn't seem to follow through. It was as though there was a blind spot in my thinking.

*

Boarding school sputtered to a close when the school called for a meeting right before the end of the year. The headmaster, me, my parents.

It was a meeting that my parents had been dreading, as it was sure to signify a change. And not for the better.

I actually had no idea what was about to come down but when they started to talk, it sounded familiar and sadly unsurprising.

I wasn't living up to my potential.

I wasn't taking advantage of what was being offered.

I didn't seem that interested in what I could make of my life.

Here at Concord, we are helping our students to become well-rounded members of society, contributing and helping others. Our girls go on to leave their mark on the world.

They said these things as I kept my head down, looking at my lap and my torn cuticles. My father withstood the headmaster's gaze with his clear blue eyes. My mother's eyes flitted restlessly around the room.

My parents were more invested in the school than I was; they had seen it as a chance for me to get on the right track and now that chance was slipping away.

They had tried everything with me, but they couldn't seem to get through.

She's really not well suited here—your money might be better invested elsewhere.

My parents held their heads up, but I knew they felt they had failed. Although they never blamed me, punished me or gave me any more lectures, their hopes of what my life could be faded and all that was left was disappointment.

Later that day, my friend and I snuck to where the cases of sherry were stashed for the graduation reception and each stole a bottle. No one noticed; everyone was busy preparing for the end of the school year.

We rode our bikes to the graveyard and drank our sherry. It was our goodbye toast to the school.

Early the next morning, the car was packed with everything I had accumulated while being away. Hung over and feeling sick, I slept all the way home to Washington.

Two years had passed, and I was barely staying afloat.

7

Yesterday's gone on down the river and you can't get it back.
—Larry McMurtry

I sequestered myself in my room in my parent's new apartment in Washington, shutting my family out.

I wrote long entries in diaries stashed under mounds of clothes in my closet.

I smoked in the closet too, stubbing out and hiding the butts.

I read *Seventeen* eagerly each month but never read an article that said to sleep a lot, drink a lot, and sleep with boys you barely knew.

There were no articles that addressed my pain or confusion and the not-caring attitude that was settling in my bones.

I read an article on how to be popular again and again.

I met my future husband that summer at the Cellar Door, on the corner of M and 34th. It was an intimate folk and jazz music club and my fake ID was given no more than a cursory glance.

The place was always packed. Lots of acts who later became big names got their start there, but I was so taken with the experience of being there and drinking, I hardly paid attention to who was on stage.

The drinking age was eighteen. That summer I was

sixteen, eyes rimmed in black, cigarette dangling between lips painted a highly-frosted ice pink.

I had perfected the French inhale and when I saw him with his sweet face and Beatle haircut, I made eye contact. We held eye contact and became inseparable. We drank beer by the pitcher, stayed until closing and fell in love. The woods in Rock Creek Park became our hangout.

Sex, smoking and drinking. What happened was inevitable.

My parents had found a new school for me for eleventh grade close to our house in DC: Western High School. When we visited, I had a panic attack—it was even bigger than the American School in Paris.

A bell rang just as we got there, doors were flung open, and a mob of kids rushed into the hallway, pushing and hollering at each other. I could feel myself shutting down. I didn't see anyone who looked like me; five feet tall, ninety-three pounds, Mary Quant hairstyle, and a mod little sundress. I could feel myself shrinking as their energy and raw teen spirit pulsed the hallway.

I was terrified at the prospect of going there, but before school even started, I found out I was pregnant.

I put my head in the sand and began to romanticize my teen pregnancy. It was going to be a way out for me. I didn't consider what having a baby would actually mean.

My parents' first thought was that I should give the baby up, to which I vehemently objected. Adopted as an infant myself, I wasn't going to give my baby up. No way would I do what my birth mother had done. I got very verbal about a subject that had been barely broached in my family.

I had scarcely given any thought to my birth mother until the time I could use her decision to rationalize mine. I twisted it all around, so I could come out looking good compared to what she had done: giving up an unplanned and unwanted child.

I had never thought of myself as being unwanted. That truth would not be faced for many years to come; better to have the special chosen baby story as the one I kept repeating to myself, year after year.

There was a very brief discussion about getting an abortion, but it was before Roe v. Wade and still illegal. You had to jump through hoops to get one. First you had to see a psychiatrist, which I flat out refused to do. Then a second doctor had to concur with the first that giving birth would do the mother serious mental harm.

I wasn't going for any of that.

This pregnancy was going to solve all my problems; I wasn't about to let it all end in some doctor's office with my legs in stirrups and a week later supposedly be back to my old normal self.

I had no idea what that normal self would look like; but I knew I couldn't face going to that new high school.

My emotions were as intense about this one decision as they had ever been. I felt I might finally have control over something.

That I thought I didn't need school anymore was just one of the signs of how irrational my thinking was. The thought that no one was going to control my body was the single rational thought.

I made angry threats of what I might do if my parents didn't agree to let me get married. I was beyond reasoning and my parents, in despair, surrendered to my tear-streaked rage.

I found out much later that Billy's father made a visit to my parents, pulling out a checkbook and hoping there was an amount that could change their minds.

He was a good ol' Southern lawyer and he wasn't going to let his eldest son's life be ruined by some little girl who couldn't keep her panties on. My father was horrified and turned him away.

And so we got married that September, before I started to show. The nuptials were performed at St Patrick's Episcopal Church where the minister Rev. Tom Bowers had just hired an African-American assistant priest.

It was the time of the Civil Rights Movement, and a pivotal moment in this church as racial and gender minorities were welcomed and accepted. When the assistant priest's appointment was announced, fifty families quit the church. We had a few sessions of counseling before exchanging vows, but we never attended church after the wedding. Maybe good things were happening in the church at that time, but we never stuck around to find out. We didn't want to have anything to do with organized religion; it wasn't our thing. I had stopped believing in God anyway.

*

We stayed with my parents after the baby's birth to get some extra help and rest. It felt comfortable there; like I was being taken care of and some of my fears faded away. Billy and I shared the guest room and after he went to work, I would rest with Kim cradled in my arms, staring at her perfect fingers and toes. The delicate features of her tiny face were exquisite. She was a miracle and I could look at her for hours. I hoped I could be a good mother and figure it all out. I wanted these moments to last forever.

Too soon, we were back in our little apartment and it didn't take long to feel overwhelmed with cooking and housework added to the mix of being a new parent. I took correspondence courses to get my high school diploma and made tuna casseroles from the *Betty Crocker* cookbook. I was going to make it work.

It felt like I had a new full-time job and I was constantly sleep deprived. When I breastfed her though, time stood still, and she and I were the only people in the universe. Only then could I put my nagging fears aside.

Billy and I didn't seem as close as I wanted us to be. I thought there would be more than:

–How was your day?

–What's for dinner?

Where was the soul connection, the nights talking about our dreams and our family?

It seemed he was content to drink beer and watch sports.

We were both tired all the time.

*

When I went for my post-partum checkup, feeling low and sorry for myself, I found out I was pregnant again. I fell into a terrible state of mind.

The doctor stood over the table, her arms folded across her flat chest, her wispy hair pulled tightly back into a bun, her wire-rimmed glasses settled on the bridge of her nose, and repeatedly said:

–You are married. Another baby is good news.

–It's not good news for me. I can't do it. I can't have another baby now. I'm not ready. It's just too soon.

I just can't do it again. Kim is great, I'm in love with her, but it's so much more than I had expected.

I'm not ready.

I don't think I can do this again right now.

I tried hard not to start crying. I was in love with my baby, feeling connected and close, nursing her as I knew my mother hadn't been able to do with me.

—You told me that breastfeeding her would work as birth control.

—What does it matter? You are married now. What are you talking about, you can't do it?

I felt I was being judged. I knew having sex should have waited, but that's hard with two horny teenagers. Lack of judgment was the deciding factor in that second unplanned pregnancy. I shouldn't have trusted nursing as birth control. Fewer than two in a hundred women who breastfeed exclusively become pregnant; I thought I would go crazy with anxiety and fear when I became the unlucky statistic.

Nothing I could say to my ob-gyn would make her understand. As far as she was concerned, another baby was no big deal.

For me, the world came crashing down. This couldn't be happening.

I can't handle this.

Those sick, panicked thoughts kept running on an insane loop in my head.

*

My head was spinning when I left the doctor's office near Dupont Circle.

I felt like I was drowning. I felt out of control. There was nowhere to go. I shut down. I wanted to run somewhere far away. If I had known better, I would have found someone else to talk to, but my pattern was to isolate and cut others out.

I wanted to look good, not be some struggling teenage mother who didn't know what she was doing. I was very careful not to let my parents know what was going on.

My ob-gyn's words stuck in my head:

–You can handle it. You are married now. Don't be ridiculous.

So I tried my best not to be ridiculous, but something shut down in me. My enthusiasm for the journey of parenting dulled.

I couldn't find the energy to get dressed in the morning, so I stayed in my pajamas all day. I had a sense of impending doom and I felt so guilty for all my thoughts.

I was sure I wasn't a real mother or else I wouldn't be feeling this way.

I drank and smoked throughout my second pregnancy and when my daughter was born, I chose to bottle feed.

Elle was sweet and easy to take care of, warm and compliant, never demanding too much of me. It was like she already knew about me and didn't want to push, to upset me with her needs.

I didn't seem to connect in the way I thought I should. I kept a distance between us. I couldn't give what I didn't have, and I couldn't name what that was.

The feeling that something was wrong with me grew. I was experiencing post-partum depression in an era that had yet to coin that phrase. They called it *baby blues* and it was supposed to be something you would quickly and easily get over.

I told myself to snap out of it.

So many things could have been different, so much could have gone another way, but hindsight doesn't heal a heart that feels nothing but the pain of mistakes made.

Postpartum depression is the real deal, with quantifiable symptoms and many cases reported each year. Some of those symptoms may include insomnia, loss of appetite, intense irritability, and difficulty bonding with the baby. Common symptoms are feeling sad, hopeless, empty or overwhelmed. A persistent doubt that she can care for her baby is also common.

Alcohol or drug problems can increase the risk for postpartum depression.

My drinking was getting heavier. So my troubles were of my own making. That's a hard truth to swallow when I wanted to blame others for the mess that was my life.

Getting over it is a lie we tell ourselves. We tell each other to forget about it, whatever it is, but I'll tell you now, that's impossible. It's really just another way of saying, Bury it. Bury it deep and don't think about it anymore.

But what happens in the middle of the night, or when you see a mother and child and a memory comes back, or when even a scent can trigger an emotion?

It's hard work keeping it all at bay, like holding back a crashing ocean wave with your big toe pushing hard against the sand. It's all an illusion and sooner or later I would have to deal with it. Just not now.

*

We needed a bigger place now that another baby was coming and so we moved further out from the city where the grass was greener. I became a stay at home mom with a nonexistent resume and a spotty work record.

I was a high school dropout with a flimsy correspondence school diploma. I couldn't keep a job. I would always quit just before getting fired.

We won't be going out drinking so often, so we'll probably save a lot of money.

We thought we were settling down just because we weren't hopping over to Georgetown to cruise our favorite clubs.

We had liked The Keg on Wisconsin Avenue where white-booted go-go girls in elevated cages danced all night. We listened to cover bands and only got off the dance floor to drink draft beer that we ordered by the pitcher. Everyone drank like us and we fitted in completely.

The nights of walking home across Key Bridge to our little apartment, usually staggering and laughing, would now be a memory.

*

God, it was the last place I imagined I would be.

A basement apartment.

I looked around the place and felt the walls closing in. It wasn't a bad apartment, even though we got nowhere near the light we had in our other place. It felt colder somehow, but I told myself in summer that could be a good thing.

There was a slider next to the dining area and we took the kids outside to play in the newly-planted grass.

—We couldn't do this in the old place, we told each other.

There were lots of young families with children there but connecting with them was impossible; they all seemed like younger versions of their parents with their right-wing politics and khaki pants. They all seemed so serious, living for the weekend. I felt like my fun was over and I had become old overnight.

Life is but a dream.

I didn't feel as though I had any control over my life, I felt like I was at the mercy of fate. I didn't see how my actions could have made my life better. I certainly didn't see how so many of the realities of my life were the consequences of my drug and alcohol use.

I wanted to be blasé, cool and nonchalant. I wanted to be someone else; a girl who could breeze through life. Deep down, I knew that wasn't who I really was.

I was eighteen, had two children under two, and was married to someone I hardly knew. I had married for all the wrong reasons, but my denial was deeply rooted in self-justification.

I actually didn't have a clue what denial was. I didn't know it was a defense mechanism that had me completely unwilling to accept the reality of my situation.

What would I do today, knowing what I know about addiction?

I know that it's a progressive disease that picks up momentum and disastrous decision-making for as long as the addict continues to use.

A domino effect set off by the first drink.

I never could have predicted it; the plan for my life was so contradictory from the way it was going. Alcohol, and then all the other drugs, took hold and the derailing of my life continued.

It goes like this: if you continue to use, things will progress and get completely and totally out of control so that what you mean to do, you don't do, and what you mean *not* to do, you do, do.

When I thought about how things had gone so dreadfully wrong, it just become easier to blame people and circumstances, rather than to take any responsibility.

On more than one occasion I looked at myself in the mirror and asked my image

—Where are you Anne?

No answer came back.

8

When you've got nothing, you've got nothing to lose. —Bob Dylan

After the girls were gone, my addiction took over.

I just didn't care.

George and I moved in together, finding a large studio apartment in downtown D.C. There was a bank of pay phones by the elevator, and the rent was under $100. The ten-story building had an impressive lobby on Massachusetts Avenue but faced the neighboring ghetto. The building's parking lot was on 11th Street and it was always a fast walk to get to the safety of the building itself.

Look straight ahead and hurry home.

I painted the kitchen two-tone lime green. I brought my boxes of books and my Danish Modern couch from the old apartment and found some chairs to go with it at the Door Store in Georgetown.

I thought it looked like we had style and the clean lines took me far from the antiques, chintzes and needlepoint of my parents' house. I didn't want anything to remind me of the life I'd had before.

George was dealing seriously now, and the living room became the business hub.

We cleaned the kilos, stems and twigs removed, weighed and repackaged into ounces, dime, and nickel bags. We set up the big brass pharmacy scale on the coffee table.

Not wanting to be thought of as some small-time dealer, George was more professional than those who used the finger measuring method. It was time-absorbing work that had us looking over our shoulders and being in a constant state of hyper-alertness and suspicion. Paranoia was the mood most of the time.

I got three jobs as an artist's model. One for a well-known abstract artist in Georgetown who wanted a model for his portrait classes, another at the Corcoran School of Art, and the third at American University for life drawing classes.

I had a favorite blue kimono with red embroidered dragons that I had found at an Asian import store in Georgetown. Stepping on the heavy wooden model's stand, I'd grind out my cigarette and take off the robe.

All I had to do was strike the pose.

I didn't have to think, produce anything, get up early, or file taxes. I didn't have to have a conversation, explain myself, or be anything other than what they wanted. I became something to draw. It was a relief.

No more strollers, diapers, and all the work of being a parent. No more cooking dinner, washing clothes and the constant picking up after any of them. But also, no more goodnight stories, kisses or random hugs. Don't think about sticky fat fingers tracing the curves of my lips. Just forget the feel of a small head fresh from the bath nestled in the hollow of my neck. Stop my brain or I'll go insane.

I was now the quiet girl moving around to the art class specifications. Just arrange the cushions and blankets for the reclining poses, change every thirty seconds for the gesture poses, sit like a statue gazing silently off into the distance until the timer would indicate a break. The kimono would go back on, and I'd light a cigarette. Everyone smoked in the art studios then. I thought it was a perfect job.

I started taking LSD with George a few times a week never thinking about side effects or even caring about what I was about to ingest. I just reached out with an open palm wanting to tune out. Sometimes we would stay home and just let it happen, but we often ventured out into the city. Outdoor concerts were everywhere in Washington that summer and lots of them were free, musicians offering impromptu jam sessions that went on for hours.

Drop then rock.

Listening to Led Zeppelin and the Doors while lying on the grass staring at stars or sun and I was on that stairway to heaven and yes, *Ooh, it makes me wonder*. We wandered around, lost most of the time, smiling with amazement at what we were seeing. We giggled and sweated and felt like we were out of this world. We smiled and gave the peace sign to people who stared. We laughed at jokes no one told and saw things no one else saw.

That year was all about drugs until it became all about race. Martin Luther King was assassinated on a spring day in 1968, shattering my hope that goodness, truth and non-violence would overcome. My daughter Elle, who I was trying to forget about, had just turned one.

President Johnson did not attend the funeral but made a statement from the White House. Vietnam kept Johnson from attending many large public events.

Robert Kennedy said, *Let us dedicate ourselves to what the Greeks wrote so many years ago: to tame the savageness of man and make gentle the life of the world.*

He may have prevented a riot in Indianapolis but not so for DC.

Everything fell apart in that one moment and the people

in our neighborhood started to loot.

I'm gonna get me some, and it was each man, woman and child for himself. Carts piled full of electronics and leather goods all rolled by and the National Guard was called in.

They lined our street and the air would sporadically fill with tear gas. We never left the apartment for those three days but crept around, laying low, not wanting to bring any attention or trouble to ourselves. Sneaking peeks out the window from our tenth-floor vantage point down onto 11th Street, wondering if the car would be okay, wondering when it would be safe to go outside. We stayed stoned; it was the only thing to do.

Before the year had ended, I was mentally moving on.

Restlessness had me looking for change. I had started to be critical of George, the way he looked and talked, his possessiveness and jealousy, and we were having constant fights.

He never took off his white t-shirt; I never saw his upper body. He might have had teenage acne scars that my fingertips sensed, but I would never know. He didn't want to talk about it.

I thought he was stupid; after all, I was an artist's model and thought the human body a beautiful thing.

He wanted to initiate conversation, but have it go the way he wanted. Without being able to verbalize it, I was beginning to want more.

With poor communication skills, I didn't know how to ask for what I needed.

Instead, the frustration would build up and I would explode. Furious that I had no voice I started to throw things to make my point, and the situation would escalate.

Constantly in tears, storming around, slamming doors,

ending with a sulking mood that I couldn't shake.

Depressed and self-medicating, nothing I was doing was working. It wasn't working at all.

9

Each day I cry. Oh, I feel so low from living high –Lady Gaga

One of our friends was a quiet man with a moody, droopy mustache who played classical guitar with long, elegant fingers.

Smart, dark and mysterious.

I was drawn to Cliff in some inexplicable way.

We soon started to talk about literature together. He turned me on to Hesse, Jack Kerouac, Alan Ginsberg, Dostoevsky and works that matched the darkness and angst I felt inside.

His dreams were unrealized, poems unpublished, and finally, a secret vice. His addiction was lying dormant for now and I didn't recognize the gnawing craving that had once possessed him. I only saw a gritty glamour, and once again, my mind was stimulated by conversations that were fueled by drugs.

The drugs were as much a part of our everyday life as food. My days started with a joint. There was always a supply and I never considered not using.

At least with this group of people, I felt I belonged. I was one of them. We all had similar problems and wanted the same thing: for the rest of the world to get off our back.

If you would just leave me alone and let me live my life, I would be okay.

Heading up the stairs to visit Cliff, I passed by the lace-curtained French doors that led into George's sister's apartment. She was a pretty smart girl and protective of her baby brother.

She had begun to suspect that there might be something going on between me and her good friend on the floor above.

I was self-delusional.

The voice in my head was hers, accusing me of being unfaithful to her brother and in that split second, a fury poured out of me. Without thinking, my fist went crashing through a pane of glass. She came rushing to the door when she heard me scream. I turned and rushed to leave the building but as I reached for the front door handle, I saw blood spurting up from my right wrist.

They called rescue and I went by ambulance to George Washington Hospital where I was sewn up and sent home. Drama was my middle name.

Everything I had heard George's sister say about me was true, except that she had never said a word.

I had imagined the whole thing and punched out that glass for no reason but my own guilt.

Filled with guilt but I didn't know it.

If I had identified it, I would have had to take some action. Instead, I blamed others for my problems.

After the French door incident, George began to treat me differently.

I started spending more time upstairs with Cliff listening to music and watching television. We saw Neil Armstrong walk on the moon through a hashish haze.

If only.

If only Billy had paid more attention to me, I wouldn't

have been attracted to George.

If only George hadn't convinced me to let my daughters be adopted, I wouldn't have such sick feelings thinking about them.

If only George were more sensitive, I wouldn't have found Cliff so appealing. Maybe I was trying to punish George because he had convinced me to give my girls up. My every thought was one of blame.

Cliff decided to move out of the city and rented a big house in Bethesda, a suburb just north of the city, and asked me to move in with him. I left George after less than a year of being together.

The house was on a tree-lined street with lush, tidy lawns and no peeling paint anywhere. It was an affluent neighborhood where I felt comfortable and safe. I began to nest and decorate, painting the kitchen purple.

He had a daytime gig at a printing company and came home tired with ink-stained hands. He also worked on the weekends as a DJ playing jazz for an FM college station.

There was always music playing. Records he brought home to listen to before playing at the station were stacked around our living room. John Lee Hooker, Miles Davis and Billy Holiday filled our space with emotion. I loved to lie in bed listening to him on the radio, feeling proud of him, he knew so much about music. It was his passion.

Without any passions of my own; I lived through whatever man I was with. A significant piece of information, but at the time I would have vehemently denied it.

At first, his heroin use seemed recreational, but that soon changed.

I wasn't aware of it being a problem; it was more of a fascination for me. How could this substance be so powerful that it made everything else secondary? I felt jealous and wanted to try it.

Cliff's old girlfriend, Angel, used to come over to the house and they would get high together and I would feel left out.

I was taking a bath and Angel came in to pee—she just walked in, that was how we all lived. We talked while I bathed, and she peed and sounded so wise. She had her shit together. I got up and stood there dripping and she told me my body was beautiful. I wasn't sure about that.

–Hand me a towel.

–You look so beautiful.

–You're kidding.

–No, I'm not.

–I want to try some smack with you guys.

–Okay, but you can only snort it. We can't have another junkie around here.

She laughed and the light caught her eyes and I couldn't read what was in them. They watched me snort it with a short straw and at first, I felt nauseous, then like I was in a slow-motion film.

The voices in my head finally quieted down, I didn't even have to try to make them go away.

I stopped thinking about my daughters.

I stopped thinking at all.

I felt superior in a way to Cliff and Angel—I wasn't a junkie because I didn't shoot up.

I didn't realize the powerful hold heroin had on me.

*

Cliff was starting to feel sick when he didn't have any, so

I began going into the city with him to find his favorite dealer, Sis, to score. Sis was in her forties, very short and compact, an afro that had no style to it, just matted and short. She had tracks on her feet and her thighs. She tried hard to keep her arms clean.

We'd head out to 14th and U which was a nasty corner of dealers, prostitutes, kids looking for trouble, and a lot of old winos.

Everyone had a hustle.

No one wanted to tell us where Sis was, so we would cruise around for a while then park the car on a side street and wait.

Someone would see us, get the message to her, and she'd appear like a holy light from some alley, slinking up to the car and the drill would start: she'd go and cop, take some off the top for herself, then get back to us.

Scoring drugs in the city was unpredictable. It was a chain-smoking, nail-biting, looking out the rearview mirror, time. We would have waited for hours, and sometimes we did. The anticipatory relief was palpable when she came into view.

After we became regular customers, we could wait at her place rather than the car where we stuck out like the suburban hippies that we were.

Her building was filled with hustlers, pimps, whores, junkies and moms just trying to raise their children and get the hell out of there.

Sis lived with an old, burned-out jazz musician, and Bo was always there, sitting on the edge of the bed, in his jockey shorts, waiting for her. He hadn't worked in years, his instruments long gone, pawned for a bag of dope. That's how it was sometimes, taking a piece of jewelry to the pawn shop to get some cash before payday rolled around. I never lost a piece of jewelry, always felt like I was helping when I handed over a gold ring or bracelet.

—Just this once, baby.

—It's okay.

I went along with whatever was happening.

I was living through Cliff and didn't even know what that meant. I was living from one high to the next.

Sis and Bo's room was always messy with cartons and bags of food from takeout chicken joints or the White Tower on 14th Street.

A cloth rigged to the ceiling was intended to separate the space, but it didn't really.

There was a small electric hot plate in one corner and a broken-down easy chair with faded, stained and torn upholstery in the other. A black and white TV with the volume turned down sat on a folding table. I never saw a clear image on the screen. Bo would periodically swear at it and try to adjust the rabbit ears.

There was a bathroom down the hall that you didn't want to have to go to.

A sagging mattress on an old brass frame dominated the space. This is where we would end up, after Sis had taken our money, scored, and got high herself before coming home. We all sighed heavily and felt better the moment she stepped into the room, just knowing what was coming next.

When we were high nothing seemed to matter anymore; the risks we had taken and the lifestyle we were sinking deeper into faded like the torn wallpaper in that dirty room. Later we'd head back to the house in Bethesda until the cycle repeated itself and we were driving downtown again to find her.

Addiction is like that.

The drug kept calling me back and I can't remember when it shifted from being a choice to a necessity. I minimized the number of times each week we made the drive to find Sis. When we went more than once in a day, I rationalized even that.

If only I could see what I was doing to myself.

If only I could see another way.

At times, however briefly, I did see.

And when I saw what I was becoming, I looked away.

*

Cliff's parents had a log cabin along the Appalachian Trail and used it as a weekend getaway. Driving out along the Blue Ridge Mountains, with each bend of the road bringing a more dramatic vista, it was a drive full of hope and anticipation. We could feel ourselves relax as the miles between us and the city increased. Out here we would be safe.

Saul and Ellen met in Cambridge during their college days. Of Romanian descent, his brown eyes would peer deep into you when he spoke. She was head of the Literature Department at a nearby private school. The whole family was quietly intellectual.

They were avid readers, and books covered every available surface in their Chevy Chase home. When you sat down to eat at the dining room table, you would have to push piles of books aside to find a place for your plate.

Saul and Ellen were nature lovers and environmentalists too. The books in the cabin were about hiking, birds and wildflowers of North America, knot tying, woodworking, astronomy, and everyone's favorite: *Stalking the Wild Asparagus.*

Cliff's father grew up in New Jersey and had contracted polio as a child in 1929. Ever since, he had worn leg braces that clanked as he walked. He was a man of intellect, yet his powerful upper body served him well. He was still able to chop wood and see to the other physical tasks that needed to be done around the cabin.

Nothing at the cabin had been modernized. They wanted to keep it the way it had been for generations.

The outhouse, downwind and a suitable distance from the cabin had been whitewashed and was covered all summer long with pink, climbing roses. Hanging on the back of the door was a faded etching of William Shakespeare. A slim volume of the bard's prose sat on the space between the two deep holes in the ground. Shakespeare in the outhouse was very much Saul and Ellen.

Personally, I was never a big outhouse fan, even one covered in roses. And I would never sit there reading Shakespeare. All I wanted was to get done and hurry out.

There was a field filled with wildflowers behind the cabin with a narrow path leading down to a stream that curved gently through the woods where we bathed in icy waters. Another stream for drinking water was down the road and along with our neighbors we hauled sloshing buckets back to our cabin.

We played chess and drank Scotch and reveled in the quiet starry nights until we had to go back to the city.

We usually went up as a family but there was one long stretch of endless grey days when Cliff and I went alone. He was trying to get off heroin cold turkey. The drug had a hold on him that was tight, demanding, and all encompassing. His work situation had become tenuous and stressful. He began to miss shifts at the print shop and his DJ job wasn't paying enough to live on.

He drank whatever Scotch he could hold down, but he was pitiful in his sickness.

I stood by helpless.

Thank God I don't have a problem like he does.

I tried to be a good nurse, but it was a miserable five days with cold sweats, hot sweats and food he didn't want to eat.

Somehow, he got through it. And we went back to the city with a piece of the monkey off his back.

10

Everybody needs beauty...places to play in and pray in where nature may heal and cheer and give strength to the body and soul alike.

—John Muir

We thought up a plan that was completely radical, entirely different.

We decided to leave the country.

I had just turned twenty-one with a sense of freedom obtained by an inheritance left to me by my grandmother.

Our loyalty for the US was floundering as the war in Vietnam escalated and we couldn't watch the news another night hearing how many boys had died that day.

Disillusioned and among the many young people who echoed the words: *War! What's it good for? Absolutely nothing.*

The protests and rallies weren't making a difference.

—We gotta get outta this place, if it's the last thing we ever do...

We wouldn't have called it fear but we were running. We knew that if we stayed where we were, doing what we were doing, something bad was going to go down.

It wasn't exactly a sense of impending doom, but all outward reasoning demanded a change of climate, somewhere warm where we could soak in the sun, someplace away from the United States.

We were too self-centered and disenchanted by the daily drama of our own lives to see a bigger picture. We had friends who had joined the Peace Corps forsaking hot showers and cold beer to contribute something to the world.

That wasn't for us.

Our outlook was geared towards sunshine and comfort and we saw Barbados as a perfect destination.

Our plane was going to leave from New York and we spent the night close to the airport. Looking the hotel room over, finding the ubiquitous Gideon's Bible in the side table, Cliff made a huge discovery.

Under the bible was a wad of bills, bound with a thick rubber band. He went in the bathroom and called me in and we counted it together.

Eleven hundred dollars in hundred-dollar bills.

We were beyond ourselves, both excited and terrified.

He had a brown leather money belt he had bought for the trip, and carefully folded the bills into it. We went down to the dining room, looking over our shoulders every few minutes, not trusting our good fortune.

We requested a table that gave us a good view of the room and then we ordered expensive steaks and fine wine. He smiled more than I had seen him smile in months. Maybe things would really change for us.

We never thought for a moment to turn that money in.

The night passed quietly but we slept fitfully, waiting for men with guns to come crashing through the door. It never happened and the next morning we boarded the plane to Barbados.

It was our great escape. We thought our problems were over.

The hot sun baked us in the taxi to the hotel. We saw children in starched, ironed uniforms, smiling and happy even though they were on their way to school. Tropical plants lined our route. Mount Gay rum was less than two dollars. And as bad memories began to fade into the clean aqua waters of the Caribbean Sea, I thought to myself, now *this* is it.

Letter home 3/25/70

After almost a week in Barbados, we took a mail boat from St. Vincent where we had been for four days. The people there are so poor, unfortunately the wealth is controlled by a few landowners; agriculture is far more important than tourism. Our hotel was wonderful, high on a hill with a little balcony off each room. The mail boat was a huge old schooner, the cargo included fruits of all kinds, soft drinks, mattresses, a refrigerator and god knows what else. It only took seventy-five minutes to get here but the channel was really rough and everyone who stayed in the cabin was seasick. At least we had the sense to stay on deck, feeling quite like old seagoing experienced travelers. Cliff and I are happier than we have been in a long time, we laugh together. I know that sounds like such a basic thing, but we hadn't been enjoying life or each other a fraction of what is possible. We are carefree children here and plan on staying for a couple of weeks.

We went island hopping to St. Vincent and then Grenada aboard a Geest banana boat with seven other passengers, sailing by night and loading bananas by day.

Bananas are the principal export of these tropical islands and being a passenger provided us with a unique vantage point of seeing how the economy operated.

Leaning over the rails we watched men and women carrying unbelievable loads of green bananas on their heads, easily walking up ramps, avoiding any obstacles in their way, and loading them below deck in the vast holds.

*

We stopped off in Bequia for a couple of weeks and stayed at the Hotel Frangipani. We became friends with a photographer from *Look* magazine who was traveling with his wife and traipsed around seeing parts of the island we hadn't visited yet.

He told us *Look* only had eight photographers on staff, compared to the forty that *Life* had, so that the articles and pictures with his byline were all his—no other contributors. His photojournalism story of the salt marshes would be part of the magazine's issue on ecology and we wrote to my parents to tell them to look out for it in the next issue.

Another couple we met in Bequia were in the Peace Corps and had been in Turkey the previous year.

We went down to stay with them in Carriacou for a week—they had a little house right across from the beach. The beach was deserted and I combed for shells while Cliff went diving.

We slept in hammocks on the ground floor and drank raw rum that burned our throats as the days slid into night.

Bats had died in the rooftop cistern and we were advised to boil any water we drank for safety but one afternoon, in a hungover daze, I forgot the precautions.

The night was spent running back and forth to the outhouse. Our hosts shook their heads, they didn't have much sympathy for me.

We had conversations about education in the islands, and I spoke of it in a letter home.

Letter home 4/8/70

Education is very new here in Carriacou, so consequently almost impossible to be made compulsory. The friend we're staying with says that only about five children in a class of forty even pass. Their parents take them out of school for weeks at a time for absurd reasons like standing in a corn field to keep the birds away or to look after the younger children. On the other hand, on large islands like Barbados, all of the children go to school where they claim a 97% literacy rate. But Barbados is an exception; most of the islands have tremendous problems. It's impossible to just lie in the sun and shop at free port stores and ignore the suffering without getting involved. We don't really know how we can help if we do decide to stay here. It's all very confusing. Personally, I had hoped for this to be a vacation. I don't think I'd like to live here for any length of time.

We ran out of money on St. Lucia but there was still my inheritance. Invincible, short sighted and impulsive, I had the bank wire money locally for a monthly draw. With a rush of independence, I felt I could do whatever I wanted. We weren't ready to go back to the US, nothing had changed, and we still had no real direction. We decided to stay on St. Lucia for a while.

Letter home 6/18/70

I received a letter from a friend from home who has been miraculously accepted into The Neighborhood Playhouse in New York to study drama. It is very exciting as they don't accept many people and those that do get in have a good chance at making it. She is very happy, as it's a dream come true for her, but I feel a bit sad, as our lives are going in such opposite directions. Her letter was brief and I sensed a difficulty to relate to me about her plans and feelings. Sara is a very strong person and having "direction" in her life is of the utmost importance. Now that she has "direction" I suppose our relationship is destined to change. Oh well, I hope that we can still be friends. I have begun to do dance exercises as I have gained seven pounds since we got here. Cliff thinks I look better at one hundred pounds than the ninety-three I was, but I disagree.

When we first got to St. Lucia, we stayed at East Winds Inn which was owned by Americans.

It was located about five miles outside the town of Castries and situated in grounds filled with fabulous tropical plants, parrots, and parakeets.

Three dogs called the hotel home and wandered around greeting people.

It was a stark contrast to the town which had been rebuilt with wide streets and new homes after a scrub forest fire had plagued the area. There was nothing charming about the town.

The grocery store had little to offer—the milk was in a tin or powdered and all the meat was frozen.

The weekly market was a different experience.

There I felt overwhelmed and confounded by the exotic and countless unfamiliar fruits and vegetables. Was it edible or perhaps medicinal? I came home with mangoes that cost only one and half cents each!

Letter home 5/31/70

I made Lobster Thermidor with the spiny lobster or large crayfish some boys had caught and brought to sell to East Winds. It was delicious even though there are no onions on St. Lucia. There are no mushrooms either, not even canned. The people that have a stash on onions are selling them for twenty cents apiece. It's very frustrating to cook when you can only find two thirds of the shopping list. Americans take for granted the things we don't have here. Fresh vegetables, fresh milk, hot running water, sour cream, AC, movies, buses. But of course, you don't have this marvelous sea wherever you look, fresh tropical air, and unlimited Mount Gay rum. So, I suppose everywhere has advantages and disadvantages.

Living was cheap and our first apartment after staying at East Winds Inn was in a building that had been army barracks when the island was a British colony.

These old barracks, named Casa St. Lucia, had twenty-five feet high ceilings, tall windows and lots of exposed brick.

We signed a lease on a big studio with a gas stove and plenty of hot water. It was only $137 a month and included all the linens and cookware. Castries had the only airport on the island and we overlooked the landing strip.

Apart from the occasional plane, it was a pretty quiet place back in those days. We found a monthly rental for a dune buggy. It was painted metallic purple and we felt like we were all set.

We hung out at local bars, talking to local people and Cliff soon found boat work. Varnishing, cleaning chrome, polishing brass, swabbing decks, cleaning the bottom, climbing up the rigging—he became an all-round boat maintenance man.

We got work on a one-hundred-and-ten-foot schooner named *Jacare*, a charter was coming and I would be cooking for them while Cliff did whatever was needed. We had no idea of what we were getting into.

Letter home 4/15/71

The charter guests came onboard the evening of the 9th; they were a high income, vodka drinking, wife-swapping group and very unseaworthy. The boat has been very badly maintained and they were very disappointed. The lifesaving equipment was from an aircraft and completely corroded and useless with exposure to salt air. She's full of rust and rot and the owners are a very weird family. He's old and a bit soft from his daily bottle of rum for the last forty years. He didn't even care about the guests and after four days of not leaving St. Lucia we returned to Castries and the guests left. They were a weak bunch but, in a way, I don't blame them. Who wants to charter a boat and spend a lot of money to find the boat is falling apart? The owners hired an engineer who is a genius and they've agreed to take us to Grenada if we work on the boat. Hopefully she should be looking 100% better in two weeks. It's really depressing to all of us to see this huge beautiful boat in such bad condition. We are ten on board now.

Life was simple: in between the gigs we found on charter boats we drank, read, swam, drank, fished, drank, ate, drank, slept and repeated. We had lamb from Australia for dinner at the bar, but fresh meat was still hard to get. There would be an occasional pig slaughtering and of course, all the fish we could catch.

Nevertheless, with a brown body strong from swimming and working, it became easy to forget the life we left behind in DC. It was easy to believe that things were different now, and hard to see the subtle ways alcohol was becoming the focus of every day.

*

We had driven one day to see the volcano at Soufriere. I'd

been complaining because we'd lived on the island for eight months and hadn't visited one of the biggest tourist attractions on the island.

—We're in a rut.

—All we ever do is go to the beach, read, snorkel, drink all day then end up at the bar. Day after day it's the same thing and I'm sick of it. I'm so bored, let's go somewhere, let's do something.

Cliff finally gave in.

We started out on the long drive. It was only thirty miles, but the roads were extremely narrow and in bad shape— many sections had hairpin curves, crumbling sides and no guard rails. The route took us into rain forest and vegetation so thick you needed a machete to cut a path through.

At a turn in the road, there might be a farmer herding goats. Or a bus painted yellow and orange and blue with curtains of beads hanging from the open windows making frequent stops to pick up passengers.

The traffic could be stopped for ages by someone trying to fix a flat in the middle of the road. The toddlers who played in the road, the women with huge loads of plantains on their heads, or heavy wooden water buckets balanced on a long pole slung across their shoulders, all ignored the cars trying to get though.

It was a production to get to Soufriere and once we arrived, there was nothing to do but walk across the caked and crusty blackened earth smelling of rotten eggs, stare at the hot lava pits, and peer into holes burning red and sizzling with fire.

And then we were back in the car for the long drive home to Marigot Bay to settle back at the bar, drink rum, and talk about the big outing.

*

Life for the islanders was hard, backbreaking work doing what had to be done to survive. They weren't getting a wire transfer from the states; many of the older ones would spend their whole lives never leaving the island. Some had never been into the town of Castries.

Once, while we were still in Bequia, a whale was harpooned and we all motored out in small boats with leaky hulls to Whale Island to watch it being processed.

The island's formal name was Petit Nevis and it was barely one hundred feet across with no vegetation or shore line to speak of.

A whale score like this didn't happen that often and when it did, it was a huge reason to celebrate. It was only a yearling, they had lost the cow, but it was still over thirty feet long.

We watched men hip high in the belly, slicing the flesh with long machetes. The blubber was cut away first and set to boil down in large cast iron pots that had been brought over by boat.

The women, and the many children who had come along, stood close by the pots. The meat was divided among the families and we stayed until after dark when some of the meat was cooked on open fires. The local rum was drunk with happy abandon until a fight broke out. The men soon resolved it, loudly and with much scuffling, and no one died. This was meant to be a celebration!

On St. Lucia, we had been to Saturday night dances where the men set their machetes outside along the perimeter of the building after a long week working the sugar cane and banana fields. At the jump up, they would drink hard and dance hard to reggae that pounded the thin walls.

Because there were so many more women than men on the island, there was lots of cheating going on and an inevitable fight would break out. The men would tumble out of the building and find their machetes and start slicing air and cursing each other. Everyone was shitfaced, but they'd be in church the next morning and it wouldn't happen again until the next weekend.

Along with our friends James and Tanya, we were the only white faces there and these dances were definitely not among the places the hotels would tell tourists to go.

The tourist industry didn't really hit St. Lucia until after we were long gone. Everything was slow to come to St. Lucia. When news of the Black Power movement hit the island, one enthusiastic man painted his front door black to show solidarity with Stokely Carmichael and the phrase he coined to promote racial pride, self-sufficiency and equality for all people of African descent.

Letter home 09/14/70

Cliff went home for a visit and he is quite disappointed with the States and doesn't understand why it seemed so important for him to go there. I guess the grass is always greener on the other side of the fence. I've missed him so much—St. Lucia is no place for a girl alone. The men here think the minute you're alone it's their cue to move in. The only safe place I've found is at East Winds Inn where they all treat me nicely as "Mistress Cliff". The big news is the great power failure which had us without power for four days but that is a minor catastrophe compared to the problems of the US. I'm convinced that the more technical, aware and civilized a society becomes, the more screwed up it gets.

Letter home 12/27/70

Now that Christmas is over I have a little more time to write. We have been going to a lot of fetes and enjoying ourselves. Last night we went to James's brother's house, it was a big family thing, age range from two to seventy. A huge buffet dinner, then the rug was rolled up and everyone danced. It was really fun when we were all in a big circle arms around each other and Brother John the priest jumping up in the center (in his robes of course). It was rather drunken but very much fun. Everyone is included, everyone dances with one another, girls with old men, little boys, other girls and by themselves if they feel like it.

On Christmas Day, we went to a fete down at the Reef Hotel. There is only one English couple living there now as the hotel is officially closed. They had lots of food and music but most of the people there were obnoxious white pseudo-yachtsmen. It wasn't nearly as much fun as the party last night.

Letter home 4/1/71

Last week our cat Chicken was badly cut on some barbed wire, in shock with a long wound from under her belly to the top of her back, gaping about three inches wide. We rushed her to the only vet on the island who is a mad butcher who cares nothing for domesticated small animals. In the process of stitching her he cut off a nipple, sewed her up with dirt and fur inside, gave her so much anesthetic that he had to give her a stimulant. He refused to give her saline solution or glucose for shock or an antibiotic for infection. She was unconscious for twenty-four hours and I was so relieved each time I checked on her and saw she was alive. On the third day, she developed signs of a putrid infection and we went to a people doctor who gave us a prescription for injectable intramuscular penicillin which Cliff has been injecting her with. Tonight, she had five kittens and after a long anthropomorphic discussion we decided to let them live and see how she and they will be. I would feel so guilty killing them even though their absence would or might make her recovery more rapid. We shall see.

The other horrible thing was when we all went over to Pigeon Island today there was a death on the beach. A twelve-year-old boy had drowned while on a school outing. I had never seen a dead body before and it really terrified me. He didn't look asleep at all; his face and body were horrible death. We are all a little hysterical tonight. I wish this letter didn't have such awful overtones; both these things affected me so much, I can't say anything else. What I saw is lodged in my brain.

Chicken just came out by herself for a quick lap of milk, she seems a little bedraggled but all right. She picked the lowest shelf in our closet for birth; it has the soft, clean sheets on it. I think she'll make it.

But I wonder, five kittens for a child, is that equality?

While Cliff was getting medical attention for Chicken, I visited the nursery. I don't know what compelled me to walk into that place, but I was drawn. I heard not one, but two babies crying. Four big brown eyes looked up at me, nine-month-old twin girls who had been abandoned earlier in the month.

I ran down to Cliff, excitedly telling him about the girls. He looked at me like I had lost my mind. My enthusiasm dwindled as I realized what I was proposing and saw his complete non-interest in the idea.

Later lying in bed, I couldn't get the faces of those little girls out of my mind, their sparking brown eyes and their hair in tiny braids with red beads topping each end. I saw their fat cuddly bodies waiting for a hug and a home.

Motherhood; I've been there and failed. I couldn't escape my past.

*

There were lots of expatriates on boats or opening businesses on the island and we soon became friends and nightly drinking companions with them.

We all complained about the problems of the countries we had left behind, the tourist economy, what kind of season was coming next, who we missed at home, and what we were glad we were away from.

The nights passed, often driving home in a blackout on those narrow roads overrun with fallen branches and straggling goats.

When the rainy season came, we spent weeks at a time holed up with endless games of chess and Scrabble, a stream of books we traded back and forth with our friends, and untold hours on bar stools.

Drinking was a way of life that everything else revolved around.

A trip to the beach meant a bag for the beverages, a trip to the store meant a stop at the bar first, and a night at the bar meant a few drinks while we were getting ready to go out.

Making dinner meant having a glass of wine, making breakfast meant having a little smoke of pot while the coffee was brewing. We usually drank our lunch. There was always someone who was drinking more than everyone else and so we looked at them and decided that nothing was wrong with us.

How could anything be wrong with us?

*

Excruciating tooth pain led me back to the states to have my wisdom teeth removed.

Norfolk, Virginia, was my father's last command and I

recuperated at the big house on Dillingham Blvd. staffed by Philippine stewards.

I discovered that frozen blender drinks went down easily and each night after dinner I would make Grasshoppers—crème de menthe, crème de cacao, cream and ice. My stay was a brief alcoholic blur, I was anxious to get back to St. Lucia.

Once back on the island, I developed an infection from the four extraction sites. Most likely I hadn't performed the oral care I had been instructed in. Forgetting and neglecting myself was becoming the norm; habits of skin care, dental care, any routine checkups were often long overdue. When the series of antibiotics was over and I was back to myself again, we decided to move.

Our new place was closer to the East Winds Inn and the rent was a lot less too. Our friend James had built a little cinder block house and they let us have it for $70 a month. There wasn't any hot water, so we had to take showers midafternoon when the pipes had heated the water; the rest of the time we heated water on the small three-burner gas stove.

Our bed was a piece of three-inch foam over plywood raised up on cinder blocks. The house had no screens and we were always finding frogs, lizards, and all kinds of insects inside. We shrugged, it was life in the tropics.

My letters home betrayed how I was really doing; they surprised me at my lightheartedness, my interests in others and all news from home. I was living in a dream world where there was little to remind me of the past, whenever any guilty thoughts did arise, I had another drink and looked at the beauty of the island.

Why didn't these bleak thoughts just go away? I felt

deceived by everything about the adoption of my daughters.

Why did moving on only happen in the physical sense; what about my feelings?

I couldn't really talk to Cliff about any of it; how would he be able to help me?

I don't know exactly when the ennui set in, the restlessness returning. Life was routine, no drama and that put me on edge.

What was wrong with me anyway?

I had an affair with a friend of ours when Cliff was out of town—we had gotten drunk and the flirting went too far. Cliff didn't respond the way I thought that he should and that hurt my feelings.

I demanded more attention than anyone could give me. I couldn't be trusted.

A hum began in the background and doubt settled in. Too much focus on the relationship and negativity took over. A blanket of paranoia weighed heavily on unspoken words and comments misunderstood.

The distance between us grew and we didn't know how to fix it. We found things to distract us.

We spent the season working, focusing on the needs of others, showing them a good time on the island, snorkeling in special coves they wouldn't find on their own, taking them up into the hills to secluded waterfalls.

We really didn't work that much as living was cheap and our needs not extravagant. The rum was in steady supply, the wineglass was kept full and our bar bill was paid right after the rent.

11

One does not discover new lands without consenting to lose sight of the shore for a very long time. –Andre Gide

A bar stool incubated the new plan.

There were so many people living out their dreams right here on St. Lucia, far away from cold winters and insane politics, working on their own boats, being their own bosses.

The charter business was taking off as more and more people were discovering the islands; why not cash in on it ourselves?

We could charter by the day or by the week to people who wanted to escape to the islands to sail, drink, relax, fish, eat, swim and shop. These dreams were not beyond our reach.

Inertia vanished as the new project developed and September of 1974 found us in Annapolis, Maryland, the sailing capital of the Chesapeake Bay.

We began our search for the perfect boat, one we could outfit and cruise down to the Caribbean to begin another new chapter.

In theory, this was a great plan. Overlooked was the progression of alcoholism which neither one of us knew anything about. We never talked about drinking, the effects that it had on our lives, how it was running our lives. We were oblivious to all of it.

My parents were also in Annapolis now. My father had retired and moved close to the Naval Academy where he had access to the library for his writing research. My mother was happily taking courses at St John's College on the *Great Books*. No mention was ever made of the obliterating wreckage of my young family. Everyone kept their eyes forward and their hearts sealed tight as bark on a tree.

My parents were happy that I was sailing, which seemed like a healthy lifestyle and still with the same man for three years, which was longer than my marriage had lasted.

–Don't they look so tan? Don't they look so healthy?

–This will be a great adventure for them, our mothers said to each other.

Things looked good on the outside and that was good enough.

Cliff's parents arrived and we all went for a day sail on the thirty-foot sloop we had purchased and christened *Calliope*. It was a cloudless day, perfect in every way. Cliff's father lowered himself aboard using his powerful upper body and was adept at holding the tiller steady as the winds picked up in the late summer afternoon.

Everyone was smiling.

Things really were okay at last.

We held our plastic cups high for a toast.

*

All aboard and underway, just before hurricane season set in. The trip was all about the timing, and if you timed it wrong, it could mean disaster. The winds were fair, and we were filled with optimism.

The charts had been purchased and studied, the galley

stocked, clothes and favorite books stowed away. The appeal of this tiny home was enormous for both of us. It was the ultimate downsizing—in sync with the disdain we both felt for material possessions.

I bought a small table loom and spools of yarn in warm, happy colors, thinking this would be a great hobby for me. I found places to stow it all aboard *Calliope*, wedged against the bag holding the spinnaker. Plans to weave when we were at calm anchorages, or better still, dockside were set aside as the night wore on to make room for drinks. One long runner wove in a traditional basket weave pattern of slate, blue, and cream lay on the table as a reminder of another project I had begun and never really finished.

Nevertheless, it helped when my hands were busy, I felt useful when I made something you could actually hold and touch. Cliff had his guitar and we both had, of course, our beloved books.

*

How could I find meaning after losing my children, letting go of them so easily?

I couldn't bear to think about it.

The demons would simply spew out, especially after a night of extra heavy drinking, a night that was full of despair and regret.

I could not be consoled.

What kind of a person could do what you did?

Glass after glass of wine and still I had no answer. No answer would come for many years and so self-hate formed layers and become part of how I thought about myself. This pattern, this rut of thinking, kept people out, and kept anyone from getting close to me, even those who wanted to be close. I didn't want anyone to know the truth about me.

I wanted to get married again. I wanted Cliff to *want* to marry me.

Didn't he want to start a family? I wondered out loud.

I had so many unanswered questions and eventually I stopped asking. I knew I didn't deserve another chance, I had blown it. It became easier to just pour the drinks, bring out the chessboard, and settle into another evening without drama, without wanting something else. The relentless wanting was giving way to apathy.

But our evenings often were unpredictable.

We might be having a nice time, but then I would take some comment the wrong way, and my feelings would get hurt and things would start to bubble up inside. The fighter I had been with George was gone—throwing things wouldn't help, I knew that. In a sense, we were safe tucked inside our little boat, insulating and isolating ourselves from the world at large. Whatever was really going on inside our heads and hearts was kept inside; we were both too fearful to let each other in.

My walls were going up and the closeness we had once felt in all aspects of our relationship were now whittled down to just the physical. He was a good man and I wanted to love him, but I found it hard not to focus on me and thoughts of what I didn't have.

What I felt most was the empty hole inside; the hole full of remembered pain.

*

Yet somehow traveling down the Intracoastal Waterway and crossing the sounds was a bonding experience as we became part of a close-knit community of shared stories, near disasters, and tips on the cruising life with the other sailors we met. We were a breed apart from the racing boat community, less concerned with weight onboard and speed enhancing tactics, more concerned with amply-stocked wine cellars and witty stories to tell after a day of sailing.

A new way of life was underway for us and after making it to Charlestown, we decided to spend the winter there. We tied up in the city marina and went ashore, getting the lay of the land.

We found the Piggly Wiggly and got provisions including alcohol which we were happy to find was sold in grocery stores in South Carolina.

We found other people planning to spend the winter there and made some new friends.

Cliff read and studied celestial navigation, hanging out with some guys in the marina. One of them worked on the pilot boat that guided big tankers around the harbor.

I wanted to do something, feel productive, so I enrolled in the local community college. Being in school felt good to me and even though it was challenging at times, I felt a renewed sense of purpose.

I was inspired by my Ethics teacher who had fostered eleven children. I easily imagined my daughters being with someone like her, so loving and warm.

She was an approachable person although I never had the nerve to confide in her. I knew that I would be judged, and I couldn't stand even to think what she might think of me if she knew my story.

I had always thought that the foster care of a baby waiting to be adopted would be very brief, maybe at most a few weeks, but she told the class that she had children for months and months. They became part of her family and she had a mixture of joy and grief when they left her home.

She couldn't help it that she fell in love with them, it was just how she was.

It made me wonder; it made me sad.

My youngest had been adopted quickly; a beautiful baby under a year was more desirable to most adoptive parents.

My older daughter was in foster care for almost a year. I couldn't bear to think about her having to leave still another home. How can a child of barely three begin to deal with those emotions? Six years had passed, and it wasn't getting any easier. I tried so hard not to think about any of it—when I did, I would instantly be filled with guilt and regret. I'd pitch headfirst down that rabbit hole with no way out.

I would pour another drink and know it was going to be a bad night. I would try to console myself that life was better for all of us this way, but it didn't help the pain. To forgive myself was something I couldn't contemplate. I couldn't stand to think about my past, yet I couldn't forget it. There would never be a way to right my wrongs. I felt completely trapped and there was no one to blame but me.

*

Two men had become our best friends. One worked at the marina and was tiny in stature, tough, rough but with a big heart, which overflowed when he drank. His best friend, and constant companion, was named Hank. They were both licensed Captains. Hank ran the Harbor Master's boat and Cal oversaw the pilot launch, *Sis*. Their friendship went way back and they were constantly together even though Cal loved to drink and Hank had been sober for quite a few years.

They'd come down to the boat a couple times a week for competitive Scrabble games, Hank toting his big red dictionary, Cal toting the booze. Hank never complained as the three of us drank and Cal kept us entertained with nonstop storytelling. The range of tides was significant in that harbor, you could come on board at seven and when you left at one in the morning, the tide might have dropped five feet. The nights ended with Hank unceremoniously tucking Cal under his arm, like an unwieldly duffle bag, and hauling him up the ladder. Cal would curse and bitch at Hank for treating him in such a humiliating way, but they'd be back a few nights later for another round.

Hank got help for his drinking problem when it looked like he might lose his pilot's license. He told us, in a serious way, how he used to drink just like Cal, but that his life had become unmanageable and he had found sobriety from a group of drunks. What he said stayed with me, even though I was nothing like Cal. If I were, I would stop drinking too.

*

Several months later we were on our way again, landing at Spencer's boatyard in West Palm Beach, Florida. Cliff wanted to get some work done, primarily a self-steering gear for the offshore sailing we would soon be doing.

Spencer's was known for reasonable prices and good work so soon we were out of the water, up on blocks to have the bottom scraped and painted.

I found a job in a breakfast spot located on the ground floor of a high-rise in Palm Beach, just across the Intracoastal. The residents were primarily aging snowbirds from New York.

It was the first time I had encountered picky and fussy eaters. Dressing on the side, crusts cut off, diagonal cuts on sandwiches, three ice cubes only, nonfat milk instead of cream, dry tuna hold the mayo—there was no end to their special requests.

Every order was a special order and although I did my best to accommodate them with a smile, it wore thin. Cliff was sick of hearing my complaints and so that job didn't last long. Anyway, the weather had changed, and it was time to begin our trek north.

We went offshore for the first leg, hoping to make better time than the traffic of other boats and endless stops waiting for bridges to open, allowed. Yes, there can be traffic on the waterways, especially as everyone begins the caravan north.

The winds picked up by midmorning and we put first one reef in the mainsail, then another, then took the main down all together. We ran for a while with just the jib up, but that too was down by noon.

Cliff used the safety lifeline as I held our course during those nerve-wracking maneuvers. My nerves were frayed watching him on the small foredeck as the high waves of the following sea that had developed made for a very unstable footing, and he struggled hard to get the sail down and stowed through the forward hatch.

He tried his best to act confident and to reassure me that we would be fine, but with no real visibility and the self-steering gear getting a trial test, we went below decks, secured the main hatch and waited it out.

We tried to rest in our bunks, still dressed in full foul weather gear, as the day turned into night. Cliff went up on deck every half hour and I watched him anxiously from below.

The waves were big enough that the cockpit filled many times, and we would watch it slowly drain, hoping another wave wouldn't come too soon. We had a little cassette deck and listened to Hot Tuna and *Death Don't Have No Mercy*.

I thought of the little prayer my father had in his office.

Oh God, thy sea is so great and my ship is so small.

Our boat was thirty feet long and sturdy, with a deep keel, but I was afraid of the mast getting ripped off, of taking on too much water, of dying out there and not being found.

The storm ended quietly, the sun came up and it was a beautiful morning, the night before seeming like a bad dream.

When Cliff took his navigational readings, we were only a bit off course and he made the corrections and we headed into the next port, humbled by the power of the sea.

We made the rest of the trip on the waterway back to Annapolis without any incident or drama. With a big sea story to tell that we had survived; giving us greater respect for those friends who had made transatlantic crossings.

Yes, thy sea is so great.

12

Wherever you go, there you are. –Jon Kabat-Zinn

Seafood restaurants lined the docks and downtown area of Annapolis and I soon found a job waitressing. We were anchored in the harbor and I rowed our little inflatable Avon dinghy to work, leaving Cliff on the boat.

The restaurant was popular and always busy. A flight of stairs led from the kitchen to the main dining room, so it was up and down, down and up with huge oval trays stacked with heavy plates.

Still wound up and not ready to go back to the boat, I felt as though I had really earned the right to a drink or two after a hard night's work.

There was a small Italian restaurant I liked to go to and soon it was a regular pit stop. A perfect after-shift routine.

Feet aching, my back sore from carrying the trays, my pace quickened as I approached Donatello's. Relief was just a few steps away.

Sitting on that barstool, I hadn't a care in the world. I became friends with the bartender, fresh faced, bow-tied, both quick-witted and easy going. Peter and I talked about a lot of things, including his love of photography and my love of writing and drawing. He knew all the best places to work and I soon had a new job at a smaller restaurant where I didn't have to carry heavy trays.

The night shift at the Dockside was perfect for me because I was starting to find getting up before noon a challenge—I was usually so hung over. I got into the routine of stopping for a quick drink before work, then again after my shift.

The chef and the bartender at the Dockside became friends, and they kept me supplied with drinks during the night. Sometimes we would go into the walk-in for shots enjoying the frigid air, relatively undisturbed for a few minutes, then back into the hustle of the busy dining room.

We all drank like this, so I never gave any thought that I might be crossing a line. That I might be out of control.

There was no normal to compare myself to. I didn't hang out with people who didn't drink like me.

*

It's insidious how alcohol can creep into your life with no awareness of it happening at all.

How did it go from being fun, to being all consuming?

Then suddenly one day you get it, with a startled knowing. You remember with a sharp, biting clarity that it hadn't been any fun for a long, long time.

Nothing was going as I had planned, but then again, I really didn't have any plans. I somehow seemed surprised by the events of my life but didn't think there was anything I could personally do to change them.

My life wasn't my own, but I didn't know whose it was.

I wanted to be spontaneous and free; I thought that a planned life was boring, static, and bourgeois. I felt somehow smug in my convictions. People thought I was aloof, but they were mistaken. The defensive air around me was a paper-thin shield, barely protecting me from the hurt I was always feeling.

I was blacking out more and more frequently and hated waking up and trying miserably to reconstruct the night before.

The time lapse of a blackout is very disconcerting; sometimes I would forget only moments of a night, other times the whole night would be lost.

The partial time lapses are technically called brownouts but it didn't really matter to me. I couldn't ask anyone directly but tried to think up clever ways to hear the stories about the night without disclosing that I was in a total fog the whole time. It was getting to be hard work, covering and lying and pretending that everything was all right. There were too many blank spots, and I started to feel paranoid about it all. What if I had done something truly disgusting and no one would tell me?

Cliff was sick of it all, he had stopped trusting me and we decided to split. I wanted to get out from under his thumb anyway. Our hopes and plans of being in the charter boat business were quietly forgotten.

His eyes looked sad and disappointed and I hated how that made me feel. We weren't connecting in the same ways anymore; I had a job onshore and he seemed content to just stay onboard and putz around.

Alcohol played a big part in our breakup, whether I wanted to admit that or not. Unable to see that I had become incapable of staying in a relationship, of working out difficulties, or really seeing beyond what I thought I needed. My self-centeredness was epic.

We got the boat appraised and he bought me out. There wasn't any point to the appraisal really, because he felt the price was fair and god knows, I *did* want to be fair.

I wanted nothing on my conscience. We behaved like adults, meaning there was little drama, and divided the small amount of possessions we had accumulated.

My parents were truly upset when they found out that Cliff and I were splitting up. They had felt secure for a few years when I was with him, they had liked him.

They don't know jack about him, I thought.

I didn't want to talk about it; I couldn't be honest with them about what had happened between us, any more than I had been able to talk about anything that was going on with me. I had one way to operate: live on impulse. If things didn't work out, I would figure it out later.

Nothing had changed.

Time had passed, that was all.

I was twenty-five now and I was still making stupid rash decisions without thinking anything through.

I can only say that in hindsight of course; at the time, all my choices seemed justified. What was going to have to happen before things would begin to change for me? I didn't really have any sense of impending doom, or feelings that the other shoe was about to drop. I was pretty oblivious to my true condition and just kept going along, gathering steam for the train wreck my life was becoming.

*

A yellow Carmen Ghia and a small apartment started my single life.

Just a short drive from downtown Annapolis, I began to live alone for the first time in my life.

To say that I was terrified is an understatement.

I was always tired after my shift at the restaurant. Each night I told myself that night would be different. But once I started drinking, I couldn't predict the outcome. When I put drugs into the mix, there was no telling where I'd end up.

I started to bring men home after work; I couldn't stand being alone in the apartment. I didn't understand any of this on a conscious level, how I was living more motivated by fear than with a rational thought process.

Lack of self-care resulted in all kinds of medical problems. This meant frequent trips to the walk-in clinic. As soon as one ailment cleared up, something else took its place.

Chronic bronchitis from a two-pack-a-day habit had me fumbling for a smoke at four in the morning when a full bladder woke me up. A chronic upset stomach and recurring colitis and diarrhea were on my list of ailments. I had earaches, sore throats, and one humiliating case of the crabs. One morning I looked into the mirror after a bad blackout weekend and saw that the whites of my eyes were a dirty shade of yellow.

I went to the bathroom and looked down to see a floating, chalky-white turd. My heart started beating hard, I knew that something was really wrong, but what could it be?

Once again to the walk-in clinic where I was beginning to feel like a regular. I was diagnosed with hepatitis and given strict instructions not to drink any alcohol at all. I was handed the prescription with a sad smile that I tried not to think about as I left the crowded facility.

I tried to cover up the feelings of shame with a *screw it* attitude. Acting like I didn't care took a lot of energy and lately I had been feeling so tired. I wanted to just go to sleep and not wake up.

I knew nothing about the progression of alcoholism, how

it had taken away my power of choice. It seemed more logical to think my problems were caused by others, their behavior, their incessant demands and cold neglect.

When Peter suggested that I could come and share his apartment, I felt a rush of gratitude and began packing. Breaking my lease was the least of my problems. I wanted nothing more than to forget about the last few months, nights when I drove home so drunk it was a miracle I hadn't had an accident. Some nights I lost my car, unable to remember where I had parked it, stumbling around a half-empty lot looking and looking, cursing and crying until I came across it and began the drive home, one eye closed to hold the yellow median strip steady.

His apartment on King George Street was filled with plants and animals. I felt safe for a while. I started to sleep better and came home after work rather than going to the bars looking for companionship.

I watered the plants, looking them up in a book and learning their names; Swedish Ivy with glossy big leaves and the Wandering Jew with purple and silver stripes. I loved the Spider plant with its babies on long tendrils, the frothy Asparagus Fern in its heavy hanging basket with the macramé hanger.

Maybe I could learn to macramé, I thought, as I read the plant book and started to feel better.

Adding Triple Sec to my morning tea or floating Kahlua on top of coffee helped me get going. I didn't know anything about morning drinking, but I was doing it every day.

The sun streamed in through the drafty old windows that wrapped around two sides of our big room. The platform bed sat snugly in the corner and for a while, things seemed almost normal.

A routine developed as I followed Peter into his darkroom at the back of the apartment. The lights would go off and I would hang over the counter as he worked, and I began to see the magic that could take place. I started taking pictures with an old 35mm Leica that had belonged to my grandmother. She had taken it to Africa on safari, and it made me happy to think of her having adventures and traveling and looking at strange and beautiful things through the very same viewfinder that I looked through now.

I became lost then found as I learned the process one step at a time. Mixing the solutions to develop the film, setting the timer and waiting, unrolling the film and hanging it up to dry, looking at the negatives carefully, deciding which ones would be worth printing, became an orderly process in my disorderly life.

Each one of the steps seemed to slow me down, and as that happened, I worried less, I thought less of all my problems, and somehow felt a strange kind of happiness I didn't recognize.

Peace.

I didn't have a name for it though, and it didn't last as the time would come to go to work and the drinking would begin again.

I wasn't a periodic drinker. I was a daily drinker and usually I would smoke pot every day too. I used cocaine, mushrooms, hash whenever it was available, but the alcohol was a constant. I never said, No thanks, or Not today.

It was always, Yes.

Saying yes to the high was saying yes to the fracturing of a relationship, yes to doubt and distrust, yes to paranoia and cynicism.

Without any understanding of the process, I was saying

yes to an increasing despair that seemed inevitable and deserved.

Soon Peter was moving out, leaving me to take over the lease and buy all his photography equipment at an unbelievable price.

It all happened so suddenly.

But in my world, people were always leaving, and things were always changing hands.

13

Having a wonderful time. Wish I were here. —Carrie Fisher

Around this time, I met a beautiful, carefree girl whose thoughts echoed mine. We finished each other's sentences and became best friends immediately.

Sunny and I connected like long-lost soul sisters and got high whenever we were together.

Her parents had a big house in Gaithersburg, Maryland, with several outbuildings sprawled across many acres and a sparkling blue pool nestled under a huge tree.

Her uncle was a thoroughbred horse trainer and all the outbuildings I never investigated were probably stables. I cared little for horses, too big and frightening for me.

No, I was perfectly content to drink and swim. We talked and tanned away many afternoons, driving back to Annapolis in her big mint green Lincoln Continental, speeding stoned down Route 50 to get to our jobs in time.

Sunny and I went up to Newport that summer and partied through a slew of hazy incidents. It was the time of the America's Cup and we followed the boats by day and the handsome Aussie sailors by night. We got dressed up to get messed up, sipping wine and doing a few lines of blow before we left the house. There were endless open bar parties and two more pretty girls were never turned away.

I was staying with a man I'd met who had a small

apartment in the carriage house of a stately Victorian on Bellevue Avenue. He said it was okay for Sunny to stay with us too and that created wild fantasies, but only for him and only in his imagination. Nothing ever materialized.

I was not interested in being anyone's girlfriend at that point and he soon tired of my antics, excuses, and the under-attention he was receiving from me. He let me stick around but I was more like the disastrous sister you couldn't bear to throw out. I was tolerated but his interest was drying up like forgotten teabags on the counter.

We drove out to Provincetown one weekend to see her ex-husband who owned a bed and breakfast. We got more coke from him and stayed up all night with new friends. Sometimes the blackouts were a good thing because I just didn't remember the humiliating events of any given night. Waking up, or coming to, with someone I didn't remember meeting was becoming all too frequent. When I wasn't in a relationship, I was out of control. I pretended that I didn't care.

Sunny left for parts unknown, and I met someone new.

His coke supply was his most attractive feature.

He worked Monday to Friday as a cook at Harpo's, a funky bar and music venue, returning to his place in Greenwich Village, New York, for the weekends.

The front door of the second-floor apartment on Bleeker Street was secured by a row of seven locks one above the other.

I saw why.

I had never been around so much coke at one time.

We spent weekends constantly high but still my cravings were never satisfied. I helped myself while he was sleeping, sneaking around his place, spending too much time in the bathroom with the water running to cover up the sound of what I was doing. I was paranoid, but not enough to stop.

He had a beautiful German Shepherd who looked fierce but was sweet and gentle. I would take her for walks when I was too high to sleep, and I always felt safe whether we were in our neighborhood or down by the piers along the Hudson.

One night out walking, I became fascinated watching a man no older than me eating out of a garbage can. *I'll never be that bad,* I thought, as I watched dirty fingers cram ends of sandwiches into his mouth. His head was turned sideways as he ate, and he watched me watch him.

I hadn't slept in two days, was still high, and probably looked a mess, but I justified I was better than him. Comparing myself to others who were worse off than me normally made me feel better about myself.

But not always. Deep down I knew that everything was a mess and there wasn't anything I could do about it. Nothing I did, nowhere I went, seemed to make any lasting difference.

I changed relationships at the first sign of things not going my way; it was a knee-jerk reaction with me. I had no communication or problem-solving skills; I didn't have the slightest idea that I was the problem.

As both summer and my fling faded away, I was ready for another geographical cure. I was sure that things would be better in a warmer climate. Sunny was in Fort Lauderdale now and it didn't take much to convince me to visit. I caught the next plane. Once again it was an impulsive decision and the weeks I spent there were mostly in a blackout. I remember her large room in the back of some man's house; we had our own entrance, but he was a frequent visitor. We all got high together and then would drive to the beach, or go dancing, or go on another wild excursion to meet up with even more fabulous people.

One afternoon as the sun hung low in the sky, a man named Steve took some beautiful photographs of me in that soft, mellow South Florida light. A fraction from carefree and happy; the next morning was just another headache, a sick forgotten night.

When I returned to Newport, the questions started up in my head: Where was I going to live? Should I go back to Annapolis or find a place in Newport? What was I going to do, who should I try to connect with, what if this or that happened? These thoughts bombarded my brain with their insistence and consistent clamor until I couldn't stand it any longer.

I looked for relief from the noise in my head in the usual way; I picked up the first drink of the day, the first joint of the day, the first line of the day. Soon my problems would lose their urgency and a new plan would be devised, often grandiose and entirely impractical, probably risky and slightly dangerous. That was how I liked it. That was how I felt alive.

I couldn't get up in the mornings if I had been drinking heavily the night before, so I tried to schedule everything I needed to do in the afternoon. For most things that worked, but not for the jewelry classes I wanted to take from a local goldsmith who insisted on an early start.

My interest in jewelry making was ignited by an intensive weeklong workshop I'd been to in Willimantic, Connecticut studying silversmithing. Whenever I found something new to be passionate about, I could usually rally, and this was one of those times. I loved living in the dorms and taking classes all day. My drinking was reasonably under control and I felt good about what I was doing. I came home with a whole new set of skills and the resolve to get my life together. Again.

The goldsmith finally agreed to give me afternoon private lessons. But one day she needed to change the schedule and I said yes to an 8:00 a.m. lesson.

The previous night I'd been out and by two in the morning, I knew I would have to stay up all night to make that early class—there was no way I would wake up if I went to sleep then.

I showed up, still drunk and trying to hide it, insisting I was fine. Forgetting to tie up my long hair, it got caught and wrapped around the power hand drill I was using. She immediately pulled the cord from the power source and patiently tried to untangle my hair from the drill and calm me down, but I pulled away and made the problem worse. Eventually freed from the drill, I couldn't focus or concentrate, and the teacher cut the lesson short, probably for her own sanity. She'd had enough of my hangover.

There was always drama around me, but I just couldn't seem to help it. Embarrassment created another layer of shame and things were escalating. Powerless to change anything, I felt a victim of my own life.

*

Later that fall during another Ft Lauderdale visit to see Sunny, we cooked up a scheme to buy a lot of coke, sell it, and realize a tremendous profit.

We had a foolproof plan and would soon have enough to finance spending the winter on the beaches of Brazil.

Back in Annapolis with more coke than I had ever had in my life and no shortage of eager buyers, things should have worked out. It's just math, right? Sell x many bags for x and soon you've made your money back and then it's all profit.

There is only one way a business plan with an addict can go.

I never took into account the massive amounts I could do myself. I had set aside what I thought would be a generous and entirely reasonable amount for personal use. But before long, I was sneaking my own little glassine bags.

I tried hiding the supply from myself. My best efforts failed miserably. Once I started using there was no reasoning involved. I understood nothing about addiction but I did understand the farce my life was becoming. Something had to give, something had to change. The fantasy of winter in Brazil gave way to an ever-growing alcohol and drug dependence.

Not long ago I dreamt about some coke. I was with my dealer and he had put out what he said would be a month's supply. I couldn't hold back my astonishment; this was a day's supply I told him. It's called a drunk dream and they used to frighten me, but now I'm grateful for the reminder. Once an addict, always an addict, even in my subconscious mind there won't be enough. One drink is too many and a thousand aren't enough.

*

Sunny's obituary didn't give any details or tell me what I wanted to know. All it told me was that she was forty-eight years old. Too young to die.

14

And when I found out what she was headed for, Mama, it was too late. –Undun, The Guess Who

I had a new boyfriend and I was crazy about him.

I was sure that he was the one.

No questions, no small talk, he didn't care where I'd been or what I'd been doing. When I found out he was married, I fell apart.

The tampons and nail polish in the medicine cabinet gave it away. His wife worked out of state a lot of the time and it took me a while to catch on. I probably recognized the clues but buried my head in the sand. *Don't acknowledge it, and it doesn't exist!*

Crying and begging, I had no shame in my desperation to win him away from her. It wasn't going to happen—his wife actually knew about me and they had some kind of insane arrangement I would never understand.

I had never gone out with a married man, it was a personal no-no, and now being with him reinforced my low opinion of myself. I wanted to believe him when he told me they weren't really together. I should have walked away.

I was afraid of being alone. I just couldn't face the four walls by myself.

I threw pathetic fits, not appealing in any way, as he would walk away from our nights together. My pleading failed. My hot angry tears got me nothing. Following him out to the street left me standing alone and shameless as he drove off.

*

One night, I decided I didn't need him to have a good time and drove alone to one of the roadside bars on Route 50 that usually had good bands.

I'm not staying home feeling sorry for myself, I thought as I brushed out my hair, permed into a halo Afro style. I knew I looked good in my oxblood leather jacket, platform shoes, makeup expertly applied.

I parked towards the back of the already full lot. Walking with anticipation up to the door, I swung it open and was hit with the full bar aroma. I inhaled deeply and felt like I was home.

There was one small problem. It was Monday and that meant football.

I was disappointed but stayed long enough to get drunk enough to forget my seatbelt rule—*if you're gonna drink, buckle up*—and took off a few hours later, high as a kite, slumped in the car's low bucket seats.

Without the seatbelt fastened, I put the car into gear and peeled out of the parking lot. Closing one eye usually brought the road into focus when I was drunk, but it didn't seem to be working this night.

When I hit the telephone pole on the passenger's side of the car, I had passed out already. The right side of the car took the full impact throwing my head against the windshield. The night was quiet with only the sounds of gentle wind in the trees. A car behind me stopped, the driver checked on me, and then left to call the police. But first, this

Good Samaritan disposed of the array of bottles on the floor behind my seat.

I had been at my parents earlier in the week as they cleaned out their liquor cabinet of various items they didn't use that frequently.

–Sure, Daddy, I'll take the Drambuie, the Creme de Menthe, the Kahlua.

With all the bottles disposed of, the subject of alcohol never came up from the police or the hospital.

No blood alcohol levels, no tox screening, no investigation, no charges, no ticket. No nothing.

Just one sad girl trying hard to kill herself without even knowing it. One unconscious girl waiting for the ambulance, waiting to be extricated from the twisted metal of the yellow Karmann Ghia nicknamed *Daffy*. Yellow like a daffodil. I hadn't had that car very long and the accident totaled it.

The oxblood jacket was brand new and they sliced it hastily away to access my right humerus which had fractured as the car imploded.

I chose that jacket from racks of soft leather in an upscale boutique on Main Street. Peter bought it for me, before he realized I added nothing but drama and pain to his life. Like a bad play that you wanted to walk out of but didn't want to call attention to yourself. He was patient; he was waiting for me to play that last scene, so he could quietly make his exit.

I came to on the table in the ER, under bright hot lights. My arm had been set but the long vertical gash on my forehead that came very close to my eyes lay open waiting for the plastic surgeon. The ER team had decided I was too young, too pretty to undertake the job themselves—it needed skilled hands. They emphasized *pretty* as if without my face I was nothing. *I'm more than just a pretty face,* I thought as I drifted in and out of consciousness on that narrow gurney.

The surgery was performed, which also included closing cuts on my scalp and chin. They did their best to fix my outsides.

—She'll heal very nicely, they said to each other.

*

My parents were in Newport visiting my sister. A big snowstorm had shut down the east coast and all flights from Providence had been cancelled. They had to rent a car to make the treacherous slow drive down I-95 not really knowing the extent of my injuries.

When they got to Ann Arundel Hospital, they found my married boyfriend in my room, calm and taking care of me.

—Thank you, they murmured squeezing his big hands. Marion, an interesting name for this very masculine African American, filled my parents in on my progress and they were thankful for his attention and concern.

After my parents left, Marion stayed. Over the next few days, he set up a vigil by my bedside.

I was in a lot of pain but had been overjoyed when he showed up. Whatever the hospital was supplying for pain didn't seem like enough. Marion sneaked in some alcohol and coke to help me get through.

Nothing ever seemed like enough, whether it was presents at Christmas when I was twelve or shots lined up on the bar a decade later. Something felt like it was missing in me, instead there was a hungry hole with an ungodly appetite that always felt ravenous. I had a constant thirst that just wasn't getting quenched.

*

My parents had raised us to accept all people regardless of the color of their skin, but I didn't fully appreciate the values they instilled in me for many years. During the sixties and early seventies, I was more hung up on my father's position in the Navy and what was happening in Vietnam, rather than their position on civil rights and how they too shared the dream of equality for all.

I was so preoccupied with our differences that I was blinded to our similarities.

As the years go by, of course, I realize that I want the same things that they always wanted; for their children to be happy, to have good health, good friends and a sense of wanting to contribute to the world in a larger way. I thought they were thinking small and now I know that it was me that was thinking small.

My self-centered fears kept my world small.

When I got released from the hospital there was the big question of where I was going to stay. I would need help for even simple things so going back to my apartment on King George Street alone was out of the question. I couldn't stay with Marion. As sweet as he had been while I was in the hospital, he was still very married, and he couldn't take me to his house.

My parents were headed back to Newport and I would never think of asking them for help.

I would never consider asking them to change their plans for me.

I ended up with Cliff, who was back with his parents for the holiday season at their home in Chevy Chase. It was the perfect place to recuperate, a sanctuary of quiet, reading, no questions asked, no third degree from anyone. They set me up in a small room downstairs, next to the bathroom and his mom's office and accepted me again as one of the family.

I'd look at Ellen as I padded to the bathroom, her straight back to me, head down, facing the long wall of books that was her life.

If only things could be so simple for me.

Everything was even more complicated as my right arm was taped close to my body to inhibit any movement. A fractured humerus was treated quite differently back in 1973; my arm was cast with a ninety-degree bend, so the elbow joint was completely immobilized. Brushing my teeth was an ordeal. I couldn't wash my own hair. I couldn't do simple things for myself like opening a can of soup. I tried wedging the can between my body and the counter, cursing when the opener malfunctioned. It wasn't worth the trouble.

The room faced north, and the steady light matched the steady decline of my thinking.

Cliff and I had sex because I was grateful to have a safe place to be, to thank him for washing my hair. It was the least I could do. It meant nothing.

Every afternoon his father and I would drink tea—the smoky lapsang souchong we both loved that was kept in a wildly-patterned tin that stood out from all the others on the shelf.

What we discussed is lost to me; he was a storyteller and had a way of making everyone feel comfortable. At my old boyfriend's house, I was being taken care of. Really because there was no one else.

Did Cliff and I talk about getting back together?

I don't remember, I was still obsessed with Marion. Married or not, I could not get him out of my mind. I wanted what I could not have and took too easily for granted the care that was being offered.

Was it love that was being offered?

So wrapped in my own drama, I didn't even try to see what was going on with Cliff. My old love treated like an old shoe, kicked off and neglected.

When I was well enough to go back to Annapolis and my little apartment, I walked through the rooms, looking at the layer of fine dust on everything, the withered spider plants hanging listlessly in their pots.

I felt lost again. In need of rescue. I went to the animal shelter and rescued a kitten instead. I named her Jubilee.

I wasn't quite sure what my next move should be. I had just been though a traumatic event and hadn't even really felt all the ramifications of that accident. With the kitten running haphazardly around my feet, I decided to cheer myself up by decorating. I painted the backroom in the apartment all white, sloppily rolling on the paint with my left hand, and made it my bedroom. My neighbor helped me out; I thought he felt sorry for me, but he wanted something.

I found white gauze curtains, a white comforter, a salvaged bureau I had lacquered white. I placed a white sheepskin rug next to the bed, so I could feel the softness. I managed to put mirrored tiles on one wall and stared at my ghostly reflection.

I now saw a girl whose arm was still taped to her body, whose head had an overly large shaved area where tight black stitches showed. I put on a slouchy hat to cover them.

Lonely eyes that looked afraid stared back at me.

I walked to the kitchen to make a cup of tea, wrapping my kimono around me, one arm flapping free, red birds on a turquoise ground. I waited for the water to boil and measured loose Constant Comment into the brown earthenware teapot. As the tea brewed, I got down the bottle of Grand Marnier. This was not morning drinking, this was a pot of tea, each cup liberally laced with the sweet citrus liquor.

I started to relax and daydream about how things would be when I got the cast off my arm, how I would somehow work things out with Marion.

Working things out involved him leaving his wife to be with me. I couldn't handle thinking about him not wanting me, so I poured myself another cup of Grand Marnier tea.

*

One night, Marion came over, to break it off once and for all, but again, I wasn't hearing what he was saying. I followed him into the street, barefoot in my kimono. Eyes rimmed red with disbelief, denial and hurt. He didn't turn back, he didn't listen to my pathetic calls; he just kept walking to his car.

Suffocating by his rejection, weak and not caring whether anyone saw me standing and sobbing as a light snow began to fall, I seethed with a hot anger that I didn't know what to do with. I wanted to lash out hard at something. I wanted to hurt something as much as I was hurting. I had no way to express or handle any of these feelings; my only relief came in drinking myself into a blackout. I knew that one thing; I didn't want to feel any of these feelings. Nothing that I could do or say to Marion made any difference at all; he was done with me. It was over whether I wanted it to be over or not.

*

It was the week after Christmas and everyone was getting ready for a big celebration.

God knows I had nothing to celebrate as 1973 ended. In my white room that New Year's Eve, I tried to feel festive with the help of Champagne and a bag of coke, but my cast was awkward, I felt unattractive, and before long the loneliness set in.

It was always like that when I drank, the more I drank the more I hated to be alone, the more I hated to be alone the more I tried to reach out to people. I called the number to get my horoscope. Aquarians would be taking charge in the New Year it said, and I thought for a while about the changes I could make. None of them seemed worthwhile.

I thought I heard voices from the living room and crept quietly in to see who was there. I must be hearing things. I called the God line and listened to the recorded prayer of how God was always there if we ask him to come into our lives, how he will lead us, and carry us and save us from the sins of the world.

It sounded too good to be true, but I knew God was just another scam for pathetic lost people. The sin part turned me off and I hung up violently. It had made me mad.

I heard the whispering again from the other room and again went down to see who was there.

The room was empty.

I turned on some lights to make the voices go away.

I felt doomed to carry feelings of loss, guilt and regret for the rest of my life which I was sure wouldn't be that much longer.

I thought about not living to be thirty that night.

I thought about all the ways I would probably end up dead. I wanted to die anyway. I looked up the number of

Alcoholics Anonymous and stared at the phone book lying between my widespread legs on the bed. I raised my glass and pushed the phone book onto the floor.

Happy New Year, I thought dismally.

*

The next day I came up with a plan: the only way I would really be able to get over Marion was to move away. Because of my physical state with the cast and all, I would need to get some help. I enlisted the neighbor who had helped me paint and decorate my room to drive a U-Haul truck up to Newport, a town I'd decided would be a great place for my new start.

He said he would drive because I promised coke and sex.

He must have thought it a good trade because he was very enthusiastic in getting my stuff into that truck and heading up I-95.

I packed the darkroom equipment, my bed, my clothes, and some kitchen stuff jammed in a box.

I packed my books—I couldn't go anywhere without my books; they gave me comfort, reason and identity.

I set aside the plants I wanted to take. I had brought the spider plant back to life with tender loving care; I had a Crown of Thorn cactus and a Wandering Jew. Those plants were coming even if they posed a packing problem.

We packed the truck together and I don't know how I would have managed it alone even though at the time, I'm sure I took him for granted. We used each other to get our needs met.

I picked up Jubilee and got out of Annapolis as fast as I could.

I was sure Marion would be sorry when he realized I had gone; when he realized I was out of his life for good.

I never thought that maybe to him I was a nightmare. That what had started with such tenderness, then passion, had become completely insane.

15

I'm nobody! Who are you? —Emily Dickinson

The apartment I found in Newport was in a neighborhood called Top of the Hill, bordered by Memorial Blvd. on the south and Mann Ave. on the east.

It was in fact the same neighborhood we lived in when I was a child, before we moved to France. Large homes, many with historical plaques on the doors and polished brass knockers, on streets with gated gardens and old beech trees.

My apartment was on the second floor of one of those old homes; the house had been converted into five separate units. The third-floor apartment was tiny, empty and unheated but I rented that too and transformed the kitchen into a darkroom with the equipment I'd brought up from Annapolis.

That darkroom was my refuge, where time stood still and quieted the relentless voices that filled my head with doubt and fear.

My apartment had spacious rooms with twelve-foot ceilings and a fireplace that was unfortunately sealed off. I would have liked a cozy fire, I thought, as I stared at the plaster square where a blaze once crackled warmth.

It was an impulse move to find a new life.

I needed the pain to go away.

It would be the next chapter in my life, right? I could start fresh and leave the past behind. I thought that taking myself away from the scene of so much recent heartbreak would take away the memories.

Once again, I fooled myself into thinking that the problems in my life had nothing to do with me. I wanted to think it was external things that caused all the disasters.

This is called a "geographic" or a "geographic cure", and it's the idea that being in a new setting could bring about a new life. It's an attempt to cure or escape the disease of addiction by moving to a different geographical location in the hope that distance from "people, places, and things" associated with drinking or using will make abstinence easier (or unnecessary).

It's the easy and oft used recourse for addicts and alcoholics who want desperately to believe that a new start is all that they need. Rather than stop and consider motives for moving to a new town, it's the quick fix, much like the drink and the drug is.

I was running away from my problems, even though I had neither clarity nor honesty enough to admit that.

I needed to keep the dreaded feelings of abandonment at bay.

It was nearly impossible for me to live in the present moment.

I was constantly regretting the past, worrying or anticipating the future. Sometimes I was like a kid waiting for Christmas, with a head dreaming of shiny new things that would bring happiness.

I was unwilling to look at how my drinking and drug use was the contributing factor to my problems, and until that day came, nothing would change.

If nothing changes, nothing changes, and I kept doing the same thing over and over.

I would tell myself I wouldn't do this thing or that thing and yet, after I picked up a drink or drug, there I was doing this and that.

I said I wouldn't drive drunk, then forgot all about it after I'd had a few.

I said I wouldn't go into a blackout, I would be more careful, and another night would become a big ugly blur.

I never knew it was the first drink that set up the physical compulsion to continue drinking, unable to stop. I always thought that if I could just have a couple, or maybe switch to a wine spritzer, I would be okay.

But when it got close to closing time at the bar, I would order two drinks or shots at a time. I never was a very ladylike drinker; I just wanted to get as much in me as I could.

Moving to Rhode Island made no difference to my addiction.

*

My parents had also returned to Newport.

With the proximity to the Naval War College, my father's old school, St George's, and the many people they had remained friends with, they still had strong ties to the community.

They rented one of the houses bought and restored by Doris Duke in the late 1960s, a big colonial painted Restoration Blue. Over a period of nearly sixteen years, eighty-three houses were saved and lovingly restored by a team of architects and skilled craftsmen. Their house, the Langley-King house, was built in 1710, bought by the Newport Restoration Foundation in 1969, and restored in the early 1970s. These restored houses had strict rules my parents happily complied with. The furniture could be reproduction but had to be period. Our family portraits looked right at home.

Stuck in my own little world, I cared little for the history of the house; it just didn't interest me at the time.

Somehow though, I hoped that being in the same town as my parents would stabilize me, anchor me, and hold me from a world that seemed so often to be spinning out of control.

I didn't really verbalize any of this to them; I didn't want to get their hopes up for any kind of relationship with me. I didn't want them to know that much about me. For years now, they had settled for what I gave; always on my terms and usually when I needed something from them.

I never saw how they longed for me, prayed for me, cried for me.

*

Instead of looking for a job, I started taking classes at Salve Regina College. It felt good telling my parents I was back in school; it somehow justified my time. Having some sort of schedule to adhere to structured my days in ways I wasn't able to achieve on my own. Glad to have someplace to go and something to do that got me out of my head, I'd otherwise be sleeping until noon and falling into a depression.

Depression was always waiting just around the corner for me.

I took a photography class and time got swallowed up working in the darkroom. I loved the precise steps I took through the process of developing film, choosing the negatives to print and then printing them. The nuance of image that was available to me was exciting and I loved everything I was learning, especially the control I had over my materials. Even to fulfill a specified class assignment, I could shoot what I wanted, making my own compositions.

Religion was a required course, but so much of what was being taught was too hard to believe.

It was the art that was saving me, but even that wasn't enough.

I rushed home after classes, relieved to close the door behind me. In my own apartment I could relax, especially after a glass of wine. I had been thinking about that glass of wine since the last class ended and I packed up my books to head home.

I lived close to Newport's many clubs and bars and most nights I would go out on foot. Fearful of having another accident while driving, I just gave up driving.

While putting on makeup and deciding what to wear I always had a glass of wine in hand. I put a lot of effort into making myself look as good as I could. Getting home was another matter; I often didn't remember any of it.

I had no idea I was having frequent blackouts; I thought that was something drunks had, and there was no way that I thought of myself as a drunk. I did think I was stupid, a victim of bad luck, and perhaps going crazy, but never did I seriously consider that alcohol and drugs were my problem.

You stupid, stupid girl was much more palatable than *you alcoholic.*

Alcohol helped me deal with life and the lies I told myself to cover up my past. I was okay as long as I didn't think about the past. I often didn't really know who was with me as I fumbled the key in the lock, trying to get into the house and up the long flight of stairs without making any noise. Memories of how I had been doing things like this in Annapolis would sometimes come to me; but I still couldn't see the link between my drinking and my behaviors.

I wanted to go unnoticed.

I wanted to be noticed.

Even with the blackouts, I do remember enough nights to make me cringe with shame. My behavior was becoming more careless and risky and the situations I found myself in became more degrading.

I went places I was ashamed to be and that only fueled my self-hatred. As alcoholism progresses, the addict will seek lower companions and I became the lower companion.

The girl takes a drink, the drink takes a drink, and then the drink takes the girl.

I'm not blaming where I ended up entirely on alcohol. There was a deep sense of not caring about myself, my safety, my very life. Had you asked me, I never would have expressed that. I would have lied and told you what I thought you wanted to hear, about how much I was loving my photography classes, how I was sure I had found my passion, how I was thinking about becoming a photojournalist like my idol, Henri Cartier-Bresson. My self-image was dependent upon what I thought you thought about me.

All the surfaces in my apartment were stacked with books; I looked through them searching for the image that would solve all my problems. I found quotes to inspire me and then decided a day later that that wasn't it. My problems were too vague to describe, a malaise, ennui, a vapid boredom that felt like a heavy cloying substrate that threatened any enthusiasm or joy for life.

Hopeless, full of self-pity and regret, stuck in my own

muck, I had no idea how to live. I didn't know where or how to begin.

A sunset could bring me to tears of wondrous rapture and an instant later, the same tears were for the meaningless, nothingness of life.

Life as I knew it.

I felt I was empty inside.

I felt like a cracked shell of a person.

16

You wanna fly, you got to give up the shit that weighs you down.

–Toni Morrison

And then one day it suddenly changed.

Waking up once again with a splitting headache, looking at my face in the bathroom mirror, seeing the purple swelling of the right side of my jaw, opening my cracked dry lips to see a tiny chip on my front incisor, this image of myself as the winter sun poured into my apartment made me feel immensely sad.

It wasn't the worse morning after by a long shot. I was alone, which was a huge relief, and I hadn't wet the bed, which had mortified me the first time it happened.

But I reached for the telephone.

I asked for help. I spoke with a woman who said if I didn't drink that day, she would pick me up in the evening and take me to a place where I could meet other people who had stopped drinking.

She lived in Portsmouth and her kindness in offering to pick up a stranger from two towns away seemed almost unreal. I wondered what she was getting out of it. I was ready when she came to get me—I had been dressed, pacing and peering out my window for over an hour, having no idea what I was getting myself into.

I was surprised to see so many young people; I honestly

thought that alcoholics were old men drinking out of paper bags sitting in the park or slumped in doorways. I listened to people who were educated, some who had been incarcerated, some old but all putting their hands out to me. A group of girls and women hovered close, giving me slips of paper with their phone number.

—Call me if you're thinking about drinking.

—We're glad you're here.

—Call me anytime.

My life changed.

It was the perfect moment for a miracle in my life. I had somehow opened myself to it, without even knowing what it was. I would be turning twenty-six in a few days and had never felt less like celebrating.

Live one day at a time.

Don't drink. Don't go to bars. Not even for a soda.

You are not alone.

You never have to feel this way again.

Don't drink even if your ass falls off.

That one put a smile on my face.

I found a community unlike anything I had ever experienced. People wanted to help each other. They wanted me to feel better about myself. They told me I would find a new happiness. I wanted nothing more than to believe them.

When they gathered and said the Lord's Prayer, my heart sunk. This was religious; this wasn't going to work for me. I hadn't believed in God in a long time; I thought faith was for others. I had become cynical and felt superior to those who would rely on a God. I knew it just wasn't for me.

Once I had seen my father on his knees before bed and felt shocked that a man who had been through wars and much hardship would have to turn to God. I thought he was beyond needing God. I thought his strength was his and his alone. My opinion of him changed when I saw his vulnerability and humility. I saw him as being more human and somehow, that frightened me.

I felt a little better about the Serenity Prayer: God grant me the serenity to accept the things I cannot change, the courage to change the things I can, and the wisdom to know the difference.

Those words were somehow calming for me. I looked at the many things in my life I couldn't change. I looked at my past and knew that I couldn't change any of it.

When I said I didn't believe in God, they said use good orderly direction as the acronym for god.

I could try that. I needed a new and orderly direction. I knew without a doubt that my way wasn't working.

I prayed to that power I had no understanding of to open my mind and my heart and help me. I had never felt such a positive force in my life that seemed to be working for the good. I crossed my fingers and prayed, yes, prayed that things could get better. I didn't really understand that it was me that could get better, not necessarily the things in my life.

I learned the difference between a bad girl trying to get good, and a sick girl trying to get well. They told me that alcoholism wasn't a moral issue, that it was a progressive illness.

This time, there was no running home to mama, no boyfriend to hide behind. It was just me, raw, vulnerable, emotional, but with a tiny sense of hope that I hadn't felt in many years.

I began to see a light at the end of the tunnel.

I started to sleep at night. No more passing out with the room spinning out of control, one foot on the floor to try to stop it. I would wake up without having to rush to the bathroom to throw up. I didn't really like to get up early, but I could do it. I began to trust that what I told people I would do, I would do.

—I'll be by to get you at seven.

I would be there at seven.

I started running. I had practically given up exercise, unless you call lying on the floor doing yoga with a glass of wine close by exercise.

I was drinking lots of coffee and still smoking, but it was starting to feel so good to be alive.

In the college classroom, I became an eager student. I came to class prepared. I wanted to participate. I didn't feel ashamed because now I could remember where I'd been and what I'd done.

The curiosity I'd had about everything returned to me. I slowly saw how drugs and alcohol had taken all my passion and ground it right out of me.

I met a beautifully coifed and made up woman with a lilting English accent who remarked, —I have been able to identify with the most improbable people.

There was a heavy emphasis on *improbable*. I slowly began to see how listening and identifying with people was helping me out of the isolation I had felt for so long.

There is a baffling mindset of the addict. We long to be included, while at the same time, we want to isolate. I was good at isolating but now I was learning to share what was bothering me, to get honest about how I was feeling. Naming my emotions was a powerful tool and I began to see how my whole life had been driven by sick emotions. My overwhelming need not to feel the pain had kept me from learning anything about myself.

And so it was for me this magical time where hope entered my heart.

Oh, God. Help me get this right.

I began to cry.

I began to tell the truth about my addictions.

I kept on crying.

I wasn't a bad person, but a sick one.

The first drink would set up the physical compulsion, so that I would need to continue drinking, even when I wanted to stop. I would drink even when I didn't want to and that used to baffle me completely.

—You're weak.

—Where's your fucking willpower?

—What is wrong with you?

I never had any answers to these questions I would angrily ask myself, and that added to my frustration.

A physical compulsion to drink made sense when it was explained to me, because there were plenty of times I wanted to just have a couple but would still be at the bar for last call.

—I've done it again, I would say, as I tried to maneuver off the barstool and walk with some semblance of decorum to the exit. I have puked in the ladies' room, reapplied lipstick and returned to the bar to order another. If only I could learn how to hold it better. If only I could pace myself, but it was always just one drink after another. If only I could stop before I lost control.

I had a mental obsession and I admitted that I was always thinking about drinking and always so sure that I would be able to think through my problems after I had a glass of wine. The wine always came first. The wine was always the answer.

They said you can't fix your own thinking with your own thinking and that made some kind of weird sense to me too.

I knew that my life was a mess because of many decisions that I'd made, and all those decisions were made under the influence of drugs or alcohol. I needed to learn how to think clearly without any substances in me. Sometimes there were so many voices in my head I thought I was going crazy, but when other people said they had the voices too, it made me feel better.

Like one guy says, –I'm not much but I'm all I've got. I'm always on my mind.

I started to feel like I really wasn't alone anymore. I might be crazy, but I had found my tribe. I could breathe a sigh of relief. I could sit beside someone shaking worse than me and tell them they were going to be okay. I was able to think about someone's pain other than my own.

They said, Keep it simple and that made me want to cry.

Nothing had seemed simple to me for years.

They said, Do the next right thing. They weren't saying this in a moralistic way, but in a very practical way. When you get out of the bed in the morning, make the bed. Now making the bed had never been on my radar or in my plans for the day, but I learned that I actually could feel kind of good by looking at that made bed.

They said go to the store and buy some groceries. When you get hungry, you won't have to go out to eat. I started with Dannon yogurt, bananas and Tab. I hadn't kept any real food in my fridge for a long time, so it was a new concept to wake up and eat something at home. With a distorted body image and always on some kind of diet, I weighed ninety-eight pounds. I slowly started to learn about getting healthy and taking care of myself physically.

The spiritual part was harder for me to come to accept or even understand, as I thought it meant I had to return to the religion of my childhood or believe in a God with white robes and a long beard.

Any mention of God could make me recoil, conjuring up all kinds of cultish fears in my head.

I felt I should be independent and that reliance on a god was definitely a sign of weakness.

The same man who suggested good orderly direction as an acronym also talked about group of drunks and I liked that.

This man had been an atheist, but he broke the spiritual part down in terms I could understand.

We were all in it together and the fact that we hadn't had a drink was some kind of miracle, and that was higher power in itself.

My way wasn't working.

Nothing could help me as long as I kept doing it alone.

Together, we were staying sober.

I could relate to the emptiness others shared, my loneliness and separation from others. I could relate to the hole in my heart and how my feelings seemed dead to me. I felt there might be a link between my spirit and my heart and the Great Spirit.

A universal spiritual force that didn't take sides sounded good to me. I wanted a force that wouldn't love me more if I were good or love me less if I were bad. I was sick and tired of being judged.

It would take many years before I could see myself without putting on the labels of good and bad; many years to see myself as a human who made mistakes but didn't have to spend the rest of her life paying for those mistakes. I slowly came to believe that I wasn't a mistake.

And so those three parts—mental, physical, spiritual—I

had grasped to be the components of alcoholism.

I soon added the sexual part, the financial part, and before long I could see how my drug and alcohol use had seeped into all the areas of my life, like mold growing in the damp corners of the basement. I didn't have any parts that hadn't been affected if I was being fearlessly honest.

I had never looked at myself in this way. Sometimes it was exhilarating but sometimes I was just plain terrified.

There was so much going on in my head and sometimes I wanted it all to go away. I learned that those were the feelings that made me want to pick up. There was a quick solution to my problems, but I constantly had to tell myself that using wouldn't solve them.

A drink will only make things worse.

Using would only bring on new problems, so I stayed sober. But sober is more than just not drinking. It's a complete makeover of a person's thinking and attitudes. I didn't see that in the beginning. I saw things pretty literally; I wasn't looking for nuance.

What I heard was: Keep it simple.

I used what I heard to rationalize my way of thinking.

17

Love is not love which alters when it alteration finds.
—William Shakespeare

Stay out of relationships for the first year and just concentrate on recovery.

But being in a relationship was just another side of my addiction; that I always ran to be with someone, often finding myself in deep and wondering how I got there.

My old behavior of acting impulsively was showing; only now I wasn't drinking. I couldn't stand the idea of having to change everything about myself. After all, shouldn't not drinking be enough?

They said that the addict/alcoholic stops growing emotionally at the age that they start using. That seemed a little farfetched to me; maybe for others, but I was different.

Today I know better.

I had never learned how to solve problems, how to think through a situation before I took action, how to resolve conflict with someone through communication, the list goes on and on.

I held onto behaviors that were immature and some of those behaviors were about using relationships to avoid being alone. I may have stopped drinking and using drugs, but my life skills were deficient.

It was hard to be alone. I couldn't stand it.

Relationships had always been my quick fix, and now that I wasn't drinking, I needed a relationship to hide in more than ever. This vulnerable feeling was my cue to look for ways to get comfortable.

It wasn't long before I met someone.

He was creative, a shop owner, and fresh out of a relationship. Everyone wore his distinctive hand-crafted jewelry.

I had continued with the silversmithing I had learned in Willimantic; I now wanted it to be my new career. I was filled with a manic enthusiasm that fueled me; no time for reason or planning or taking things in small steps. I threw myself into making a new life.

I set up my workbench and tools in a cooperative gallery on lower Thames, just beyond the tourist foot traffic. Along with a potter and a sign maker, my studio took up the north corner with a window to the street. The work had me fully engaged, but with a budding relationship I would leave the bench with tools strewn about and work half done to meet Patrick for a coffee or go for a drive.

I would settle into the low bucket seat of the sleek black Corvette and he would turn up the sounds and we'd be off.

I didn't know how to take care of myself, grow my business, set attainable goals and actually achieve them. I was wishing and dreaming but not really working. I was blind to all of this and was just excited that I had met someone like him.

I wasn't drinking but I was still doing things my way. My insane thinking rationalized using drugs when they presented themselves, maybe some musty, acrid hash from Afghanistan, some special Peyote buttons from New Mexico, and the last time, cocaine.

I was completely sure I would never touch coke again. I held it responsible for my insanity those final months before the last move to Rhode Island.

I knew that whenever I did coke, all bets were off, and I wouldn't be able to do anything until all of it was gone. It gave me a high like no other; making me energetic, euphoric and invincible. Ready to take on the world, full of false confidence. But I always ended up feeling paranoid, jittery— a head case.

Coke wasn't for me. It had ruined my life.

One hot and humid afternoon at Patrick's house, we were hanging out with another couple, laughing and fooling around.

I walked into the kitchen from the adjoining bathroom and there it was on the kitchen table.

On a placemat.

Eight neat rows.

Four people.

Two fat lines for me.

The rolled twenty came my way and it was as if I had never been away from the stuff.

There was no conscious period of thinking.

I hadn't thought at all.

I just used.

The thinking came immediately afterwards.

The full, expansive meaning of my actions hit me heavily, weighing into my chest.

This is what they have been talking about.

This is what powerless is.

This is what being defenseless against the first drink or drug is all about.

They had said, in an irritating way, that at some point

there would come a time when only a power greater than myself could keep me from picking up.

I guess the power had been in the coke and in me as an addict.

I felt high, but I didn't like it.

I rushed out of the apartment into the summer heat, wanting to escape myself. Walking along the sidewalk, I could sense a steady buildup of fear. I felt out of control, my heart seemed to be beating too fast. This too shall pass, I hoped, as I made it back to my own apartment. No place felt safe that day because of the crazy thoughts that were spiraling inside my head. I didn't know how to shut it off.

I couldn't believe that I had used without even thinking—even though I knew it was the one drug I had to avoid at any cost. I felt as though I was completely crazy.

Yet, somehow, when it was in front of me, I went straight for it. It gives me insight as to why people relapse so easily; why it's suggested to stay out of bars and away from the old friends getting high. They say it's like going to the barbershop and just sitting there day after day. Eventually you're going to get a haircut.

In the days that followed, I tried to find peace.

I would get into my 280Z and cruise around Ocean Drive, but the wide expanse of the Atlantic that usually filled me with calm, looked dark and ominous.

I went for long runs, counting my steps and thinking a four-count mantra as I traveled through neighborhoods far from my own. I was trying to run away from my thoughts. My crazy thoughts would be the death of me.

How did people get clean and stay that way?

How could they have fun without being high? Every day felt like a new experience to me. My thoughts, feelings and guts were in a Petri dish waiting to be examined more closely.

–What are your motives with this, Anne? a friend asked.

I had never thought about motives in my life.

It became a question I would ask myself.

My feet would hit the pavement and with each step I would try to shut up the monkey in my head.

Get the hell away.

Let go and let God.

Please stop this shit.

Thy will be done.

Help me, help me.

Step after step, mile after mile and I'd be sweating and breathing hard and feeling sometimes that there might be a tiny chance that I wasn't going crazy, that I might be okay. That my life was good, that the sun sparkled on the ocean like I'd never noticed it before, the rich rank scent of seaweed rising up and filling my nostrils with an aroma I couldn't get enough of.

And so I restarted the process of recovery. I had a greater sense that I wasn't in this alone. I started to trust the things I was hearing; that I would never have to feel this way again.

I learned that my feelings weren't facts, and that my feelings might actually change. I always thought that if I was in a mood I would be stuck with it, it would last what felt like forever and doom me to my sad same guilt about the past. I can't change my past. I still didn't understand that healing would come when I learned I could think about it differently.

That part of it could be changed.

That what doesn't kill you can make you stronger.

Patrick stopped drinking for a while and my fantasies about our relationship ballooned out of proportion. It would be so perfect. I gave in to the daydreams and let a thick mist blanket over the reality.

He hadn't been divorced long and wasn't even close to settling down or even having an exclusive relationship. I had my blinders on and only saw what I wanted to see. Any inkling of the truth would throw me into denial and my make-believe story.

At the end of that summer I became pregnant. My birth control had failed for the first time in nine years. Was it a sign? Was it meant to be? Those thoughts were quickly replaced by the old, cold fear that locked down my heart.

I had my chance at being a mother and failed.

How could I succeed now my fear questioned me?

It was out of the question.

A friend lovingly took me aside and a tentative conversation began.

She asked me if I would take the time to do some work and make a real, grown up, thought out, rational decision based on truth rather than my emotionally wrought fear-driven thoughts.

I didn't know how to do that, and I cried some more. I didn't know how to think, I was too filled with emotion and somewhere I heard my father saying:

–Annie, just think.

So I did as she suggested, locking myself up for the weekend and writing out columns of people in my life, my fears and my worries, and my resentments about them all. She saved the last column for the unborn fetus, so I could write in a more detached way.

I stayed at home, sitting at the blue banquette in the corner of the kitchen, and I wrote.

I wrote on my bed, ashtray by my side, pausing to smoke, slow down and think.

I wrote in the living room, staring at my books full of information but no answers. She told me that the answers were within me. She told me that I would find the truth within me.

When I was finished, I was so surprised. Surprised at the clarity and peace I felt inside. Surprised at the joy and happiness I felt, overwhelmed by love for this miracle in my body, this gift I wanted to nourish and cherish and birth and love close and always.

I knew in the deepest part of me that I could and would be a good mother, that I was loved, that I was forgiven and being given another chance. It wasn't over for me, I hadn't used up all the grace I would ever be allotted. Grace filled me now and I went to my friend and told her the good news. I wanted to tell everyone of my happiness and joy. But first, I needed to sleep. I was emotionally exhausted, drained from digging deep and finally doing the work.

Patrick wasn't as thrilled as I was with the news of my pregnancy.

He wasn't ready, didn't yearn for a family, wasn't ready for fatherhood. I translated that all to mean just one thing: he didn't love me enough. My thinking was that if he loved me, he would want to marry me, be a father and live happily ever after.

My hurt feelings immediately made me protective; the walls went up, the communication stopped. I couldn't let him know how I actually felt. I thought we were the perfect couple, I kept my hurt inside.

That perfection of what and who I thought we were lived in my own mind; the fantasy of how it could be. How it really should be I thought angrily. Artistic, sober, creative parents doing the right thing for their child, giving that child everything that she needed, so that she would never know loneliness or sadness.

It wasn't to be.

We parted ways, meeting for a brief Christmas reunion where he gave me a black chemise, a red boa, and a long cigarette holder. Where did these gifts come from and why did they make me feel like crying?

I tried to smile, sitting cross-legged in the middle of his big bed, my belly a tiny swell barely discernible. Are these gifts worthy of the mother of your child I wondered from some unspeakable part of myself? The part of me that had no voice.

I continued to smile, and he smothered me with kisses and wrapped his arms around me. It wasn't what I wanted. It was real all right, but his desire for me didn't match the feelings I longed for. I felt so lonely, so sad in his embrace. I felt a part of me starting to go numb and I wasn't sure what my next more should be. I didn't have any answers or clear direction.

He baked some fish in the oven, laying foil in the pan for an easy cleanup. We had never even been to a restaurant together, I thought, as the white flesh broke apart between my tongue and my teeth.

I swallowed hard, pushing it all down.

I didn't spend the night.

That was the last time we were together.

18

The most common way people give up their power is by thinking they don't have any. —Alice Walker

The winter wore on and lugging bags of groceries made my back ache. I would sink into a chair and sip a cup of tea, and sometimes I would worry about what life alone would be like when the baby came. I got some child-rearing books and gave myself pep talks.

You can do this.

Be grateful that you've been given another chance.

One day Rob stopped by to help me out. He was a friend of a friend.

—Help her out. She's alone and pregnant. You could develop a friendship with a woman where sex wouldn't be an issue. Help her go to the laundromat, shop for groceries, push that vacuum around her apartment.

My friend thought that my pregnancy meant I wasn't attractive or tempting as a woman.

He was all wrong.

Rob was young, fresh-faced with a grin that spread across his face like sunlight burst from behind a bank of clouds.

Suddenly blue sky was everywhere. His humor, his optimism, his boundless energy and his total concern for my wellbeing touched some longing deep inside of me. He was adorable, attentive, willing and available.

It did and didn't surprise either of us that a romance developed. We were both longing to love and be loved.

Long talks into the early morning left me feeling that here was someone who thought like me, someone I could trust. And when he thought that we should be together, I couldn't think of a single reason not to.

But why was he so insistent on a complete overhaul of my belongings? He convinced me that we were on a new path and I should let go of the past. It sounded okay in theory, but it was hard to get rid of so many old things. He took a broad eraser to my past while I wordlessly stood by.

Boxes of photographs from St. Lucia and Washington and sailing with Cliff and our friends all went into the trash. One picture that I loved had me standing at the edge of a wall near Soufriere in St. Lucia, the vista lush and expansive behind me, the Caribbean sparkling in the far distance. I'm wearing a pink and white cotton pareau knotted simply around my small body, my long blonde hair lifted by the wind, my dark eyes looking at the camera in a straightforward way.

Why I didn't simply put all those mementos in a box and tape it shut is beyond me, but I did as Rob asked. I dumped the books he thought too trashy or provocative, like the *Story of O* and *The Last Exit to Brooklyn*. The clothes he didn't think were appropriate, like a favorite sheer plum blouse I'd found in a Georgetown thrift store, went to the donation bins. Little bits and pieces of things I once liked, that had once defined me, were gone.

I didn't see how easily I was letting him take over and direct my life.

I thought instead of the mess my life had become, how hopeless I had felt a year ago, how much I wanted a new life.

With no idea of how to get my needs met, my emotional immaturity kept me submissive and silent.

Once again, I was becoming the chameleon, ready to blend into the current situation. It has always been thought these specialized creatures change their color in response to temperature and light, but newer research indicates these color changes express their moods, not just to camouflage themselves.

Of course, I didn't know this about myself, and was appalled when accused of being *like a chameleon*. One time my mother said it; that I was always changing myself to fit with my new friends, or more usually, a new boyfriend.

–You change your hair, your clothes, your mannerisms and figures of speech, the music you listen to. You even change your favorite foods, colors, songs to match whatever they like.

I denied everything she said.

I forgot how I could lapse into an English accent or mimic whatever accent the person I was talking with had. I considered it to be a talent, not a maladaptation to my surroundings. She really pissed me off, but maybe she came a little too close to the truth and I hated how that made me feel.

A social chameleon will mimic other people's behavior, so that their behavior passively changes to match that of others. There is an unconscious change in the person's self, as they constantly struggle to fit in with their environment, or the people around them. They present different versions of themselves, depending on the situation. With such a fluctuating identity, developing a strong sense of self is made even more difficult.

I had coffee with a friend at her little apartment on Bellevue Avenue. The conversation turned to Rob.

—I'm worried about you, Anne. You're so ready to surrender your life to his and give up yourself for the sake of the relationship. You just seem to live for him. You've made him the center of your universe and I'm not sure that's good for you.

I looked at her and I said:

—So what? What's wrong with that? Being a self is overrated.

Deep down I wondered if what she said was true.

I deferred to him, his wishes, and his way of thinking entirely. I wondered if the mistakes I made as a teenager and my relentless need to do things my way had turned against me now. I had trusted myself at one time and look how that had turned out. Maybe, I thought, it would be better for me if I let someone else do the thinking.

I wanted what he wanted.

I wanted him to be happy.

I wanted him to love me.

I thought that meant that I would have to do it his way.

*

The birth itself had been wondrous, with my closest friend being my labor coach.

We had been to all the Lamaze classes together and we were prepared.

I was going for all-natural childbirth this time, no drugs for me. I wanted nothing to dampen the experience. I wanted to feel everything. I wanted to leave the dim memories of drugged and painful births far behind me. The past was gone, and I didn't want to think about it at all.

I couldn't have felt more supported and loved, but this friend also cautioned me to slow down with my new relationship.

I didn't want to listen to her.

I thought she was trying to control me.

She had a husband and wasn't alone anymore while I was so completely afraid of being alone.

And what about *my* chance for happiness?

I was afraid that this might even be my last chance.

I was afraid that being a single mom was going to be much harder than I thought.

I didn't see what she saw and after the birth, I pushed her aside. I thought I didn't need her quite so much anymore. I didn't see the warning signs. I only saw and felt Rob's interest in me.

I didn't understand why I needed to look at myself anyway. I didn't want to face feelings of fear, inadequacy, or feeling overwhelmed. What could I really do anyway about those areas of my life?

Many of my friends were getting into group therapy and saying how much it was helping their sobriety, but I didn't want to go there. What was the point of going back to my childhood, those nightmare teenage years, to revisit the things I was trying so hard to forget? I was willing to look at behavior that I could relate to alcohol, but that was about it. I couldn't see how it was all connected.

My underlying fear of revealing my deep secret to any group would leave me vulnerable and that thought was unbearable.

Who could ever understand what had happened to my two daughters and the messy unraveling of my life? How would I ever be able to explain all that and not risk being judged?

I had never fully examined the guilt I felt about giving up my daughters. I tried, but would be so overcome with emotion, I had to stop. I couldn't bear the feelings. I never worked through the shame I felt for the choices that I had made. Instead, I got busy and distracted, and put any really deep healing about my past out of my thoughts.

*

Jessica was eight weeks old and I was back at the shop. She was nestled in her carrying bed and I was at the bench, looking over the paperwork for the commissions I'd completed before she was born, assessing the display cases of the jewelry I had designed and made.

The inventory was a little sparse; I had been so obsessed with my new relationship and my new baby that I had neglected my work. The birth, adjusting to a newborn, breastfeeding, wanting to do everything right was taking up all of my time. Mostly, I felt exhausted.

I hadn't been there long when Rob stopped by with a coffee from the Franklin Spa. He remembered the cream and the Sweet'n Low I liked.

He wanted to talk about getting married, how he didn't want to just be my boyfriend.

He went on about the benefits of being married and raising Jessica, how he would adopt her, how we would have health insurance from the job he had at the hospital. How could I possibly admit to him that a boiler operator wasn't the career I had in mind for my husband? That just sounded judgmental, elitist, so unaccepting.

–I need time to think. I have a new baby. It's too soon to have this talk.

–You're procrastinating, he said. –You have difficulty making decisions.

He was right about that.

The outcome seemed so heavy to me, what if I made the wrong decision? I had been making wrong decisions my whole life.

I didn't trust myself and taking responsibility seemed too huge.

I knew with my whole being that next to getting sober and saving my life, having Jessica was the best decision I had ever made.

My life was changing in small but miraculous ways and I wanted to savor each moment, each new day filled with such hope and promise.

–You're procrastinating, Anne, he said again.

–Don't you want what's best for Jessica? Don't you want her to have a real father? Don't you want her to grow up in a normal family? Marry me. Make a decision now.

The morning wore on. I wasn't getting anything done with him bullying me. It was hopeless to even think about trying to work. I was starting to get a headache and while my tools sat idly on the bench, the sun rose higher in the sky. Jessica woke up and I nursed her in the rocking chair we had brought down to the shop.

–I'm going back up to the Spa to get our lunch. Make a decision and tell me when I get back.

So, it was a bacon cheeseburger from the Franklin Spa that called it.

He had an undeniable gift of persuasion. His rational thinking and explanations all made perfect sense. It was impossible to argue with his logic. His reasoning was solid and I didn't want to risk losing him.

He relied on my guilt.

He relied on my fear.

Sadly, I felt there was no other way; it was simply easier to say yes.

Now he would stop.

It would all work out.

It would be okay.

He would provide for Jessica better than I would be able to alone.

I wouldn't have to ask my parents for financial help.

There must have been a deep sense of shame, being a single mom in 1977. There must have been a deep sense of abandonment when Patrick didn't want to marry me. I didn't want to face any of those feelings which swiftly led me to a downward spiral of thinking.

Alone I was nothing; someplace inside me I truly believed that and my destiny played out that summer morning. From the start, there was only one way this would end, and it would be his way.

*

The wedding took place in Jamestown when Jessica was five months old. She wore a long white gown of the softest cotton; I wore an off-white wool dress I made myself.

Rob's father forgot his sports coat and made do with a burgundy velour pullover. I pretended it didn't matter as I looked at Daddy's blue blazer and regimental tie. A friend played the guitar and we ate finger sandwiches and toasted with sparkling cider. Our wedding night was interrupted for me to express breast milk into the bathroom sink of the historic inn we had booked.

I couldn't wait to get back to my baby.

*

And so, our married life began.

We lived in a seven-room apartment in the two-family house we had purchased. It was the worst house on the block, but we got it for $30,000 and a low interest rate. We used the money from the sale of my 280Z for a down payment. Rob thought that car was too impractical anyway.

Our house was on the wrong side of Broadway, but Rob could walk to work and the rent from the first-floor tenants paid the mortgage. The boiler had to be replaced immediately after an emergency flooded the basement. With no landlord to call, we were suddenly real homeowners.

I loved the classic glass-fronted cabinets in the kitchen. We painted the walls a warm creamy tomato sauce bubbling on the back-burner kind of color. A color that meant this is the heart of the home. Never would I have guessed the role food would play in our relationship.

I stayed at home while he was at work underground in the vast boiler room of Newport Hospital.

I would clean all morning and he would often stop in for lunch. One day, swiping his index finger along the top of the fridge, he picked up a fat worm of dust. No words were necessary; the raised finger said it all.

I hadn't passed the white glove inspection.

Not even close.

I had no clever retort; I had nothing to say.

As soon as he left, I made myself a plate of French Toast with gobs of butter and dripping with syrup. It filled the gaping hole for a moment as I was eating, but it marked the beginning of using food to push down my feelings.

Was I angry, or was I ashamed?

I only knew that I hadn't measured up to his expectations.

They say that drinking is a symptom of an underlying problem. Alcohol was no longer part of my life, but food seemed somehow to protect and insulate me from the emotions that signified a loss of control.

*

We decided to stop using birth control and have a child of our own.

We were thrilled when we found out we were pregnant with twins just as Jessica turned one. Twins ran in Rob's family.

I was painting a rainbow that covered one wall of the bedroom that was going to be Jessica's. I was standing on a ladder adjusting my balance to accommodate my changing center of gravity as I approached full term with the twins. I was happy in this pregnancy, but hurt by Rob's lack of interest in my growing belly.

—Your skin is so taut it looks like you are about to burst.

I began to cover my body when he was around, carefully closing my robe to protect myself from his gaze. I couldn't figure out what was so different from the last pregnancy, when he looked at me with delight, wonder and lust.

Now, I was very aware of the extra weight straining my back muscles, the need to pee so frequently, the restless nights trying to get comfortable. He didn't think it was cute that a coffee cup could rest on the shelf my belly made. I could detect annoyance or maybe contempt from his glances, almost furtive, as he quickly looked away.

Seth was born first, then Lilli four long minutes later. She seemed to rise straight up through my pubic bone to face the world standing. Nursing two infants felt phenomenal. I was made for this, cradling them like jostling puppies, eager and warm and covering each other with their bodies. I felt like Mother Earth; entirely purposeful and significant.

This then is what I can do and will do well.

Beneath the façade, darkness lived.

I gave up more of myself than those possessions he wanted me to get rid of. I didn't even know it was happening. The significance of tossing out things didn't register; I just wanted to make him happy. It was easier than having a fight. I didn't want my home filled with angry words, words like I heard coming from the apartment below us, voices escalating, doors slamming, and bursts of meaningless hatred.

Our downstairs tenants were now having regular fights and no amount of banging on the floor with a broom would make them stop. Listening to the muffled arguments was so upsetting. The occasional violent outburst of completely intelligible words was unnerving.

No, I wouldn't live like that.

I knew no other way but to just be quiet and agree.

Be pleasant, be compliant, and do not make waves.

Do not disturb the waters.

Keep things calm, do it for the sake of the kids.

*

I minimized the issues in our marriage, and when a fight began, Rob quickly won. I tried harder to be the sort of person no one could complain about. I pushed my body hard to get back to pre-pregnancy shape and when I looked good on the outside, I thought that was all that mattered. I wore the clothes he suggested for me and wouldn't dream of doing otherwise.

I strove towards Steve Martin's famous line:

–It's better to look good than to feel good, and dahling, you look marvelous!

Yes, looking good was what mattered I thought as I stuffed myself with leftover food and then exercised triple-time the next day.

I switched one addiction for another and didn't have a clue about what was going on or why I was doing it.

Lost, found and becoming lost again.

Life was moving fast, and I was losing control. I just needed to try harder.

Having three babies under three left little time for my jewelry. It wasn't the kind of work you could do in small time increments and get anything done. I had set up the small room off the kitchen as a workshop, but the tools gathered dust and I eventually packed them up. A dull resignation set in as I put away the wire cutters, pliers, files, metals and gemstones that had given me so many hours of concentration, creativity and fulfillment. All my darkroom equipment was long gone too.

My old workroom was redecorated as an extra bedroom and a friend stayed for a while, helping out as a nanny in exchange for room and board. I tried to accept the new arrangement. I held on to a new resentment.

I felt like every other young mother; that I had no time

for myself. I never looked for ways to continue with the jewelry making; it was a creative outlet that I really enjoyed but I didn't know how to hold onto it when it wasn't being supported by my husband. He told me I wasn't being practical. He told me I was selfish.

A row of plants topped the shelf at the head of the stairs. We had renovated our attic, adding two bedrooms, a large master and a smaller room for the twins. After another argument, I pushed all the plants off that shelf; back to my old ways of acting out instead of verbalizing what was going on with me. The plants went crashing down the stairs, dirt spilling, shards of terra cotta everywhere. He started to throw the furniture around the room, overturning a chair.

—You want to mess things up? I can mess things up. Just watch me. Who do you think you are? You have nothing, no education, no skills, and three children. Without me you are nothing.

He pinned me to the bed, the vein in his right temple throbbing as his face reddened with anger at the nerve of me trying to act out against him.

After that terrifying moment, I became even more careful not to anger him or do anything to set him off. I watched carefully for signs that he might be in a bad mood and I would try to be extra nice.

Stay clear. Don't argue. Don't get him started.

I cleaned up the mess so there was nothing left to see of the struggle between us. I got rid of the evidence that all was not perfect in our lives.

Maybe I did settle. Maybe my life felt amazing ninety percent of the time. In the end, all my energies went toward not drinking and my three children.

19

We're not meant to be perfect. It took me a long time to realize that.
                                                            –Jane Fonda

When my friend, Kathy, who had also recently a baby wanted to get in shape, she came over and we exercised together.

I designed a sequence of exercises and showed her how to do them with good form.

It felt good to sweat, to move in tandem with someone, to be appreciated by someone.

I felt like I had something to offer.

She said I inspired her to work hard and encouraged me to teach a class.

I placed a small ad in the *Newport Daily News* after getting space in the lower level of Emmanuel Church, where there was a huge room with hardwood floors and basketball hoops at either end.

My exercise class met all summer long, three times a week. Rob urged me not to tell anyone this was the first time I had taught, but to act as if I had been teaching for years.

Taking his suggestion, I acted as if I had all the confidence in the world as I started up the music—a mix I had recorded one song at a time from vinyl onto a cassette tape —and led the class through a warm-up, standing, sitting, lying down exercises and a stretchy dance-like cool down I had drawn from my experience in yoga and modern dance classes.

The class grew through word of mouth. One of the girls, who had become a good friend, had a brother-in-law who was building a racquetball club in Middletown. Leslie also told me that the manager wanted to have an exercise program. I approached him—again coached and rehearsed by Rob—and became an independent contractor providing group exercise class to the members.

1980 was really an exciting time, the beginning of the explosion of aerobics into the exercise world.

There were no sport specific shoes at the time and we exercised barefoot. I read Dr. Cooper's *Aerobics* to understand the benefits of cardiovascular conditioning and learned to calculate my exercising heart rate.

A look through the Jacki Sorensen method led me to design an approach that was less dance, more athletic, more geared to attract men as well as women. Less girly and more physically challenging.

As soon as I could do five men's push-ups, I added them to class. No one was doing men's push-ups in exercise classes and I got the reputation of having hard classes—hard in a *good, push yourself to the limit*, kind of way.

High impact all the way, the harder the better and when the room was filled with fifty people and the music was deafening, I felt happy.

I designed a variety of classes, made countless tapes, and watched the program grow.

Capitalizing on the trend, Reebok came out with the *Princess* aerobic shoe that we wore with leg warmers, shiny tights and matching headbands—no baggy T-shirts. It was all about looking fit. My goal was perfection.

I don't know how this became my goal. I never felt even close to being there, no matter what anyone would say about how I looked, it was never good enough in my opinion.

The critical eye I had towards my body was relentless.

It was difficult to sustain the strict diet that kept my weight around one hundred and four pounds.

I was always hungry. I kept thinking I hadn't found the right combination of foods. Was I eating too many carbs, I wondered? I cut out carbs. I followed the grapefruit diet, the hardboiled egg diet, I went to Weight Watchers.

I was starving myself and I didn't know it.

I would be good for a while and then something would happen, and I would use food to feel better.

I became a binge eater.

I knew nothing of emotional eating and didn't see how food had become a substitute substance for me. It never worked and then I would overcompensate with exercise to try to get back to that perfect place, the place that I could never maintain.

All weight loss seemed precarious; I didn't trust myself around food. I felt empty, and at the same time, feeling so stuffed I was sure I would never eat again.

My unhealthy relationship to food was insanity, but I didn't see it. I could never look at the underlying reasons for the starve/binge style that had become my normal way of eating.

Any extreme behavior can be a red flag indicating unhealthy behaviors. Exercise bulimia is a subset of the psychological disorder called bulimia in which a person is compelled to exercise in an effort aimed at burning the calories of food and fat reserves to an excessive level that negatively affects their health. This disorder is caused by a number of factors including low self-esteem, perfectionism, and the culture's obsession with thinness.

An opportunity presented itself to open my own exercise studio. A space had become available and we took it. I was tentative, but Rob thought it would be a sure thing. It would fill a niche for women that would be unique. *La Vie* offered a variety of classes and I trained instructors to my high standards, after adding many more classes than I could teach alone.

After receiving National Certification, I felt a growing confidence in myself and looked to offer more to our clients. We had a specialist who brought the newest technology to the studio to measure body composition and I was thrilled when my number showed 15% body fat. The average woman has between 25-31% body fat and I knew I didn't want to be average.

I worked hard to be in that low range; often teaching extra classes just to burn off any excess calories I might have eaten. Counting calories and constant weighing became obsessive behaviors.

When we went out to dinner with friends, Rob would count the fat grams on my plate, but then order desert. It would drive me crazy that he could ruin a meal like that. I didn't want the reality of what I was eating to be so clearly described to me. I had so much resentment, but I stuffed it all. I literally stuffed it. I would have told you another story back then, how great my marriage was, what a close family we had. I wanted it to be true.

What was really missing in my relationship was the freedom to be honest and be accepted for myself. Everything would be analyzed, and then Rob would offer the fix. Most of the time I just wanted to be heard; I wasn't looking for the fix.

—Don't fix me. Just listen to me.

What would have happened if I had said that?

My fear kept me from even considering it.

Rob was not comfortable when conversations or events took an emotional turn. He tried to redirect and often told me that I was overreacting. I didn't know how to stand up to him; it felt like a proposition that would threaten whatever comfort level I did have. I didn't want to do anything that might cause him to fly off the handle. I became good at reading his moods and matching them to my words.

*

There's a big difference between being in recovery and being dry.

The massive heart-aching problems that active alcoholism surrounded me with and the desire to drink were gone.

There had been enough days and years without any alcohol or drugs that I began to think I was okay without the need to be around the people who had helped me in the beginning.

I didn't think about drinking.

I didn't think about *not* drinking.

I didn't have a problem anymore.

I got so wrapped up in my world that I forgot that one of the basics of a happy sobriety was to be there to help someone else, as I had once been helped.

I forgot the flood of relief when I first made contact with someone who drank like me but had found a way out.

The hands that reached out to me holding slips of paper with phone numbers were forgotten, along with the hugs and the hours spent talking about how to live now that I wasn't running to get high anymore.

I lost touch with the woman who had guided me in the beginning, the one whom I ran my problems by before I reacted.

Often, she would tell me to just wait. She would tell me to ask my higher power for direction. She told me that I wasn't alone and that I didn't have to figure everything out for myself.

Somehow that all shifted, and I now thought I had to be self-reliant.

The prayer and meditation aspect of my recovery had also been transformed.

Opening and running my own aerobic studio and teaching up to fifteen classes a week took the place of the runs that had been a way to quiet my mind and connect with a power greater than myself. No longer was the sound of my footsteps hitting the pavement the noise I heard in my head. Instead, the cacophony of self-criticism was continual.

My head was filled too with the soundtracks of the tapes I made for the classes. I couldn't stop the noise and only knew I was too busy to take the time to meditate. I had orders to fill for the workout clothes we had started to carry and marketing strategies to plan. Overwhelmed became the feeling I started each day with, counting income against expenses filled my head as I tried to get to sleep. I've got to make this work was an all-consuming thought. I was on my own again, and I was feeling isolated.

I stopped praying, not as a conscious decision, but it just lost its priority.

It was easier to eat some junk food and then exercise harder to make up for it the next day rather than honestly looking at what was bothering me.

Emotions built up and then got stuffed to a place inside I had no desire to visit. Once again, I didn't want to go into the past. It became about how to avoid the pain. I lit another cigarette, opened another Tab and tried to figure it out.

And then there were still the old issues of my daughters buried inside.

I had never found a way to move forward. I would tell myself continually that I had done the best thing for them at the time, but the hole in my heart wouldn't go away. I hadn't tried to make amends to my daughters; just thinking about them brought me to tears. I had no idea how I could ever right that wrong. There was no way I could ever feel forgiven and accept myself.

It was one more thing I had to just live with. The idea that I could one day be free from my past was inconceivable. Maybe that could happen for other people, but not for me.

When I first got sober, I did make many amends, mainly to my immediate family. I had tracked down some of the others too and did feel a sense of freedom when I admitted my wrongdoings to them. I was truly sorry that I had hurt them and wanted to know what else I could do to make things right. The response was always the same: just stay sober, that's the best thing you can do for both of us.

Making amends to Kim and Elle was never going to happen because there was no way that I could ever see it happening. Never in my wildest dreams could that part of my past be healed.

This was probably the biggest lie my disease told me.

Having a spiritual life took a back burner for the same reason as missing meditation. I was too busy. I didn't reflect and see how my personality traits were still there, minus alcohol and drugs.

I wasn't willing to really look at myself to see how immature I still was. I didn't see that my sulking covered the fear I had about so many areas of my life.

I knew my marriage had problems, but I just blamed him.

All of the feelings of being inadequate and the fears and growing resentments were personal problems I thought I had to manage. I was trying hard to change myself and it just wasn't working.

I forgot that the hole inside could only be filled by a loving spirit; I was losing my way and not seeing the signposts.

When my relapse eventually came, it wasn't a surprise as I look back at all the events.

Being in recovery is an action term; it means there are things to be done on a daily basis to keep my thinking free of self-pity, fear, dishonesty and resentment.

Consciousness happens by being present and during the ten or so years that preceded my relapse, I just wasn't there. I was going through the motions of living, but I had lost the spiritual connection which gives real purpose and meaning to life.

I was doing the best I could but left to my own devices, I was stuck in the hallway between the hell that had been my life and the real joy that was yet to come.

Life was better in so many ways, but I was still short-changing myself.

My self-esteem never reached a healthy level, no matter

how thin I was, how great my house looked, or how well my family was doing. I was going about it in the wrong way, trying to make the outside look good when what I needed was an interior makeover.

I kept hitting the same wall.

I was too afraid to go deep inside.

20

Your vision will become clear only when you look into your heart. Who looks outside, dreams. Who looks inside, awakens. —Carl Jung

We moved to Jamestown when Seth and Lilli were almost three and Jessica was starting kindergarten. My father helped us buy a house after seeing that we were clearly outgrowing the apartment in Newport.

The house had been built in 1900 as a summer cottage in a neighborhood known as Shoreby Hills. There was no insulation, no basement, but lots of big, bright rooms and a glorious full attic with high ceilings and two windows on both the north and south side. I envisioned the kids using it as a giant playroom and creative space.

As we walked through our new home, I could see there were things to do. Rooms to be painted, window frames to be replaced, a bathroom that could be remodeled. We were ready to plunge in.

The master bedroom was huge and we added a little balcony to it when the new back deck was built. It was the perfect place to sunbathe on warm spring days when the garden below was dotted with daffodils and tulips after the masses of crocuses had faded.

We found a sailmaker to make a canvas screen in a deep classic green which we attached with turn clips to the railings. The two-part clip was stainless steel and expensive, but it gave the look we wanted and stayed secure even in the highest winds blowing off Narragansett Bay.

I was busier than I'd ever been with my big house, new business, and three small children.

The gardens I never had before became my creative outlet. I poured over books of garden design, drawing plans at the kitchen counter and deciding which plants would work best in each location.

There had never been so much open space for the kids to play and I would sit on the big back deck with a coffee and watch them on the rope swing.

I had more than I had ever dreamed of.

I didn't think anything about my sobriety.

I didn't think about our lack of any financial plan.

Learning to save, to make a household budget, to plan for future emergencies were skills neither of us had learned. It was all about instant gratification.

Shortly after Rob and I were married, I took over paying the bills.

He'd had minimal experience with banking, so he would bring home his check and I would deposit it. If we didn't have the money for something, we'd charge it.

He developed a taste for designer labels and the high-end shops of Newport. He was tailored for the perfect blue Calvin Klein blazer from the Narragansett Clothing Company. He looked incredible—as handsome as any model I proudly thought. With big dreams he wanted to dress and look the part of the man he wanted to become.

He quit the hospital job to go back to school; he had the GI bill from his two-year stint in the Navy and it seemed like the smartest thing to do. He was going to college at the University of Rhode Island to get a degree in finance. It would surely lead him to the riches he'd dreamed of as a child. Our hopes were so high.

*

When the stock market crashed in 1929, my father was thirteen. I don't know how much his family was affected by the Depression, but I do remember the passbook savings he diligently started for his grandchildren. He'd walk along the cobblestones of Thames Street from his condo at Brick Market Place to the Bank of Newport to make a weekly deposit of $5 into each of their accounts.

Daddy maintained those passbooks until my marriage ended and then turned them over to me so I could use the money for bills and groceries. I'm sure he never expected that would be how the money would be used. His aspirations were higher—perhaps the seed of a college fund, or a down payment on a first vehicle.

It seems such a waste, all those walks to the bank, year after year, to have those accounts wiped out in a few months.

Yet he never made me feel that I was doing the wrong thing. He supported me in the best and the worst of times.

I should have looked for someone like that, but those qualities make up a man's character and aren't always visible. I didn't recognize Rob's insecurities, and distorted self-image until it was too late.

*

We were invited to a cocktail party at a sleek, modern home on Ocean Drive, filled with everyone who was anyone in Newport. The kitchen was swarming with help preparing the hors d'oeuvres. There was a nanny in charge of keeping the smallest children from being underfoot. Everything was so smoothly organized.

I stuck close with the few people I knew, making small talk and holding my sweating glass of club soda and lime.

I tried hard not to compare this family with mine, they just seemed so put together. On the wall beside the stairs were framed family pictures: on skis, on boats, everyone looked so happy. There was a twinge of envy and I didn't want to be that kind of person. Let me be satisfied with what I have, but in that moment, I was uncomfortable as I watched the activity around me.

We had been at the party for a while and I hadn't seen Rob for some time. I finally spotted him, off to one side with a boy of about ten, the older brother of our daughter's kindergarten classmate. They were having an animated discussion. His face was open and relaxed, intently involved in the conversation.

Why was he wasting time talking to a kid? How would that help him develop business contacts, or even friends? You won't be golfing with this kid; you should be talking with his father and his father's friends.

Our first cocktail party became our last.

I felt like we were on the outside looking in.

The drinking scene had nothing in it for me; it was just a reminder of the past, the endless repeated stories, the leering grins, the faces too close for comfort. The cigarette smoke and the smell of scotch were just part of a life I didn't belong to anymore.

We were on the fringe of the social scene and a lifestyle I been raised to be a part of. All of it had been lost through my addiction. I wanted not to care, and in a way, I was relieved.

It felt like being dumped by a boy I said I never wanted anyway. A perverse feeling of wanting flooded me with confusion.

*

Our world narrowed down to three couples.

One couple we became friends with after we had met individually.

Angie was one of my first clients at *La Vie* and we connected immediately.

Our husbands had met on the golf course. His no-nonsense Germanic outlook was the perfect match for Rob's budding pragmatism. They were two perfectionists, birds of a feather.

They both drank but didn't seem to care that we didn't, and we started spending time with them.

Our sons became best friends.

If only everyone could be like us, our husbands thought, the world would be perfect.

Her bruises told another story, but that was something I didn't see at first.

The second couple was down to earth and eventually we became closest to them.

Their two girls were the same age as our kids and Friday night became family nights, the two families gathering for pizza or pasta, switching back and forth between the two houses. One night there was a lobster relay race on the kitchen floor before hitting the boiling water. We entertained ourselves in the simplest of ways.

We shopped together, one year getting the four kids matching jackets before that became not so cool anymore. The kids performed plays they wrote while we talked endlessly in another room.

We felt so relaxed with them; people we could be ourselves with.

The third couple was native Newporters, laid back and entrepreneurial.

Leslie had been at my first exercise class, back at Emmanuel Church.

I can't remember a single conversation, but sinking back into the sofa at their home, the refrigerator covered with family photos, a pleasant disorganization, our kids racing around together, jumping for hours on the trampoline next door, their dogs always around, we felt like we were with family.

Rob and Mike had the same December birthday and we would sometimes celebrate at the Canfield House where there was always a huge Christmas tree in the center of the dining room—everything sparkled and shined with hope on those magical nights.

We started the tradition of putting our Christmas tree up on Rob's birthday. We wanted to establish lots of new traditions for our family, something our kids could count on. We intuitively knew that whatever could bring us closer together would be good for all of us.

Our hearts were in the right place—we wanted a home that celebrated being together, a home that wasn't like the lonely place we had both been raised in.

*

When did my inside become so different from my outside? When did my feelings become unmentionable?

When did it become so difficult to access my emotions

and share them? If it wasn't a positive feeling, maybe it would just go away.

Forget the past.

How could I ever come to terms with my past, just accept it for what it was, forgive myself and move on?

This was something I spent a lot of time thinking about, but I kept it to myself.

This wasn't anything I could discuss with Rob; it was clear how he felt about my past. He didn't look back either and neither of us ever discussed what had come before.

Instead of a deep compassion for what we had survived before our paths crossed, there was a heavy door closed on it. This created a deeper rift between us and life became only about daily operations.

*

Years later, my mother recalled an Easter dinner. Sitting down at the table, Rob made a comment about the shade of lipstick I was wearing. I'd broken away from the hot pink I always wore to try a sheer red. *I like it*, I had thought as I applied it earlier.

—It doesn't look good on you.

I rushed upstairs to change it and came back to the table as if nothing had happened. I would do anything he wanted—he just had to say the word.

My mother was silently infuriated.

She looked at the blood that had pooled on her plate by the roast lamb and wanted to pick up her knife and stab Rob's hand.

Instead, she poured glass after glass of wine from the carafe Daddy brought to such dinners.

She remembered Rob's comment, but what I

remembered was her drinking. It was easier to look at her and find blame, than look at my own actions and attitudes.

I couldn't even stand up for myself and defend my choice of the color of a lipstick, but the lipstick was just a symbol and I was years away from understanding that.

Much easier to quietly and smugly think what a bastard he was.

21

Take care of all your memories. For you cannot relive them.

—Bob Dylan

My sister Marjorie lived less than a quarter mile away from our house in Jamestown. She and her husband and a band of animals lived in my grandmother's old house. *The Quarterdeck*, situated right on the bay, was steeped in family history and memories. Its backyard sloped down through unspoiled meadows to a rocky beach that stretched from Taylor Point in the north to the town landing.

The summer visits we had made as children to *The Quarterdeck* always seemed too short.

We wore old Keds faded to the color of clouds and soft from countless washings down to the beach we called the rocks. They protected our feet from the countless periwinkles, mussels and barnacles which covered and clung to the slabs of shale.

We spent hours playing in tidal pools, waiting for the tide to rise and form a bathing pool, a small area with a bottom of finely crushed shell that felt good on our feet. It was only then that we took off our sneakers and threw them up to higher rocks.

A heavy bell mounted on the side of the house close to the kitchen door was rung when lunch was ready and we'd amble up through cornflowers and Queen Anne's lace and our mothers never worried about deer ticks.

Just when did Jamestown become so overrun by deer?

Now we check everyone's legs carefully when they come inside, because we're on the lookout for signs that could lead to Lyme disease.

It all seemed so much less complicated back then.

Mr. Nunes took care of the gardens for my grandmother.

He was a small, stooped, dark-skinned man who seemed to be permanently kneeling. He walked eyes down and back rounded, his wrinkled-chestnut face grinning and showing several missing teeth.

Pushing his wheelbarrow forward three feet at a time, weeding, clipping, deadheading, and clearing, he tended those gardens with devotion.

He was probably my father's age but seemed much older as he moved silently from one part of the property to the next, from the beds that circled the driveway to the heavy peony bushes by the garage. I loved their giant pink blooms and we brought them inside in big bouquets to place on the dining table only to see a stream of ants crossing the polished wood a few hours later.

Memories like the long queue of cars waiting for the ferry to Newport have stayed with me. The twenty-minute ride was exciting, being out on the water, watching the shoreline get smaller and smaller, the journey holding the promise of an adventure every time I stepped aboard.

The early morning ferry carried men in suits with briefcases, their newspapers held up for reading as the ferry cut through the stretch of bay, leaving Rose Island with its lighthouse to port, passing Fort Adams at the entrance to the inner harbor. These businessmen had no interest in hanging over the rail like me, running up and down from the lower deck like me, or skipping from the bow to the aft railing like me. They rode the ferry every day to work. No big thing. The secretaries though, leaned on the railing smoking cigarettes, letting the wind whip their hair and smelling the sweet salt air. And when the ferry approached the dock and the deckhands threw and secured the lines, they would comb their hair back in place and check their faces in tiny compacts before going ashore.

There was an occasion when I was about fifteen, walking home from the ferry, the last one of the night from Newport. I'd been with friends and couldn't afford the trouble I'd get in if I missed it—again.

It was a moonless night, no street lights once I turned onto Bay View Drive, and every noise in the bushes put me on high alert.

My eyes adjusted quickly to the darkened road overhung with a canopy of trees and thick shrubs making a sound screen for the houses set back from the road.

Our driveway, with its crushed bluestone, worn thin in spots, felt hard against my bare feet compared to the smooth pavement of the road still holding heat from the August sun. I tried to walk along the edges of the garden hoping for softer grass but found only twigs and stones thrown from the car wheels.

I was shoeless because I needed to get inside the house without being heard; I had been drinking with my friends and didn't want my evening's activities revealed. I was a sneaky girl, and even then, there were secrets to be kept.

Another lifetime, so long ago.

No more secrets.

22

The price of anything is the amount of life you exchange for it.
—Henry David Thoreau

Rob and I didn't have a budget for savings, for college, for home improvement, not even for emergencies.

We lived paycheck to paycheck, relying on credit cards and the trust fund from my grandmother.

Every month I got a check which supplemented my earnings from teaching aerobics.

When there was a need for a larger sum, I'd set up an appointment and wait in the restored eighteenth century colonial in Newport, with its antiques and Oriental carpets, flipping through the Wall Street Journal, and making small talk with a pleasant gatekeeper.

Eventually I would be ushered into a book-lined conference room where a principal of the firm sat behind a heavy mahogany desk.

It felt just like my parents' house, and the sum I asked for always seemed to be a little too much.

It felt like asking my father for money and I had to continually remind myself that it was my money.

Ask nicely, justify your needs, and they will give it to you.

*

Years earlier, Rob said he knew a way he could increase his income by $3,000 a month. I was all ears. We were having dinner with friends, a grown-up meal with the kids happily playing downstairs after a pizza feast from A1 on Broadway.

Kathy made a dilled *blanquette de veau* from the *Silver Palette* cookbook and we were anticipating it eagerly.

No tuna casseroles for this group; we loved to cook and feast with each other on gourmet meals. It was the eighties and heavy cream and fresh herbs were in, paired with conspicuous consumption.

Lately, I had been worrying more and more that our lifestyle was draining the trust fund.

I couldn't see a way out; as hard as I worked at La Vie teaching aerobics, I wasn't making much beyond the break-even point. The extensive and expensive remodeling we had done to install lockers, showers, a bank of sinks, the subflooring, the carpet, the expanse of mirrors covering one wall, the sound system, the advertising to grow the business; that money was gone. With over forty classes a week, I was paying trained instructors, a person who watched the kids in a little nursery and double-dutied to help clean. My expenses overshadowed my income.

I took another bite of the *blanquette* and put down my fork to hear what Rob had to say.

—If I stayed at work two nights a week and made cold calls for two hours, I could generate enough business to make an easy $750 a week.

—Why don't you do that, then? I asked tentatively.

He swept my question aside by a rant on the importance of family and then deftly changed the topic. We moved on and I thought it was forgotten but when we got home the volcano erupted.

—How dare you question how I do my business? You don't have a clue how my business works.

Then it was onto my education, or lack of education, my studio and how poorly it was doing. I tried to defend it as we had grown to over two hundred members. But things got turned around to be my fault and I sat there, soaking up the blame, letting it sink deeper and deeper.

I was put on the defensive and it didn't even matter what I had to say. His jaw tightened, and I knew not to bring it up again.

I really didn't dare say anything.

Once again, I felt like I had to walk on eggshells.

Once again, I felt our marriage was far from the partnership I had so wanted.

I didn't understand what was behind the anger; his driving need to control and create the perfect family.

I couldn't possibly talk about my past with him and any thoughts of taking action to find my daughters. I was too afraid of his reaction. I could hear all his arguments against a search.

I had lost touch with my women friends and we were isolating more and more as a family. I retreated into a shell, keeping a happy face on the outside, and hoping no one would notice.

I knew enough of his past to believe he had his own demons. His father had died before he was two and when his mother remarried, he and his sister weren't accepted by his mom's new husband.

Something unspoken had happened to him when he was a child, but I never knew what it was.

He had his secrets and never allowed himself to be vulnerable with me. It would be a sign of weakness; I would have loved him less. Any show of emotion made him uncomfortable.

–You're exaggerating.

–You're overreacting.

These were the comments I often heard and so my reaction was to further shut down. I stopped feeling safe enough to express my feelings. Sometimes I just wanted to talk, to vent, to get the feelings out, but it was only a cue for him to start on ways he could fix it, fix me.

There is a pattern to a relationship with an emotionally abusive person. I had become someone who stopped trusting my own judgment. I stopped having an independent life; instead my actions were being tracked and my whereabouts were always known. I was told, in a very sarcastic way, that I was too sensitive and too emotional. My accomplishments were belittled, and affection was withheld. I was accused of being stupid, selfish and it seemed I was always saying I was sorry. I wanted desperately to figure out why he was warm one minute, then cold the next. His happiness became more important than mine.

Why didn't I see the red flags all around me?

*

One day, on an errand, an ad came on the radio before I had shut the engine off.

Lonely? Confused? Depressed? Suicidal? Call to talk before you do something to hurt yourself.

They were a nonprofit group called *The Samaritans* and they were looking for volunteers to begin a training program that was starting the following week.

I sat riveted, listening to the radio.

A single voice on the other end of the phone might be enough to help a person change their thinking.

When I ran into a friend, I excitedly told her what I had heard and how I thought it might be just what I needed. I repeated the whole thing again to Rob when he got home from work that night.

Let me go somewhere I can feel appreciated, where I might be able to offer someone a little bit of hope.

In a way, I'm surprised that he agreed to let me do it. Yes, *let* me. That's what it had come to.

The Samaritans wanted one shift a week and then one overnight a month with a one-year commitment.

The training was about active listening and much protocol as to not getting personal with the callers or disclosing any information about yourself.

In other words, let them talk, keep the focus on them and how they're feeling. Talk about future plans—people who have plans for their lives don't kill themselves.

On the phone were real people and they were hurting. The phone lines were busy all night with three volunteers taking calls; calls from people I thought of as lonely drunks. Sad stories of child abuse, sexual exploitation, alcoholism, addiction, disadvantaged people dying to talk to someone about the rotten way their lives had turned out. Everyone had a heartbreaking story.

No one I talked to had a plan to kill themselves; they would talk themselves dry for the night and then call back a few days later. So many repeat callers; you'd get to recognize their voice, be able to tell how deep into the drinking they'd gotten.

It was too intense for me to listen in a detached, objective way. It didn't feel like it was making any difference at all and I got in the habit of stopping for fast food after a shift; feeling restless and edgy and hoping a doughnut or a burger would take my head somewhere else.

I didn't want to think about the stories I had been listening to. Driving and dripping cheesy grease from a soft floury roll, cream-filled doughnuts spilling their filling into my lap as I drove from downtown Providence home, where my family lay sleeping, their ears innocent of all that I had heard.

I didn't know what to do with all those feelings. I didn't feel adequate.

I hadn't made the connection between what I ate and put into my body and my feelings, so I didn't know that each sugar doughnut only fueled my despair and set me up for more cravings. I didn't want to look at the phenomenon of craving and admit that the food had replaced alcohol and drugs, and that I was now medicating myself on a regular basis with sugar.

I should have stuck it out, but it was too much to handle. I took everything I heard to heart. I internalized their pain so when Rob suggested I stop doing it, it was easy for me to walk away.

I didn't last the year.

Once again, denial was calling the shots.

23

True wealth is of the heart, not the purse. —Og Mandino

Raising children has a way of letting parents subtly shift the focus from their marriage to their children.

I think you have to make a real effort to give the couple you once were some attention and not let the parents you have become overshadow the things that brought you together.

Rob had adopted Jessica when she was less than one and the twins followed before she was two. He was the fun parent as well as the disciplinarian. He could be in the street behind our house teaching tricks on bikes; then giving a big lecture complete with diagrams and drawings on how you have to make something of yourself and your life. Big on timelines and goal setting, he drove those values into his kids. We listened to Zig Ziglar cassettes in the car on family drives.

Sometimes those standards were just too high to live up to. I felt like I was trying to better myself and always just missing the mark. I stayed in the background as a parent; we couldn't be equals. I had to give in to what he wanted or else there would be a fight, and the last thing I wanted was to have our children see us fight. There was no conflict, so no one learned how to resolve conflict.

I do regret not standing up for myself.

I was just too afraid of what he might do.

I was afraid that he would leave me.

I was afraid of being alone. I had stopped praying or having a real spiritual life that could sustain me. Once again, I felt like I was on my own trying to handle situations that were well beyond my scope.

*

Rates for borrowing money rise and fall and whatever the rate was in 1989 wasn't a factor in what happened. The cost to borrow the money never came up in my mind as a reason for or against the idea.

Everything had changed since we were first married in our way of managing money; the shift from me to him happened as his need for control increased. I relinquished the reins without even a conversation; it was obvious that he knew more than me about money matters. He had only to point to the financial statements of my exercise business. I had lost my will to fight, what difference would it make anyway?

After all, he now had a degree in finance and was working at a global financial services firm as a stockbroker.

He came home one day with the answer to our money problems.

He'd done the research, and the papers had been all drawn up.

How much we'd be borrowing against our already mortgaged home, the term of the loan, how the increase to our monthly payment would proportionately be quite small.

How it would give us some breathing room, maybe we could finally do some things to the house, pay off the credit card debt, take a vacation.

I started to feel really uncomfortable.

I was in the laundry room as he rushed in with the papers in his hands. He couldn't wait to show me what he had come up with after a trip to the bank.

I carefully folded a T-shirt and put it in the pile with Seth's other clothes, admiring the neat stacks and feeling proud of the kids for taking those piles and putting their clothes away. I didn't have any chores as a child that extended beyond picking up my room.

I never saw my mother push a vacuum around or dust the furniture. We had a housekeeper who made sure my clothes were taken care of.

I wanted it to be different for my children and we had taught the kids to bring their laundry downstairs, sorting the lights from the darks.

We all cleaned the house together as a family on Saturday mornings before we set off for the day. Rob did the vacuuming and then the kids washed the tile floor with sponges on their hands and knees.

Everybody participated for the two hours it took to clean the twelve-room house. It wasn't perfect, but it was very much a family affair as we went over baseboards, mirrors and everywhere dirt and dust collected. Everything had to look good.

The four walls of the room seemed to be closing in as Rob loomed over the threshold holding the second mortgage papers that he was sure would instantly solve our problems. All I had to do was sign by the yellow post-it note.

–How could this big influx of money really help us now? I wondered aloud

It seemed like it would only be a Band-Aid, covering up a

much more serious problem that needed some deep attention.

–We need to figure out ways to reduce our spending.

I had an overwhelming sense that what I was feeling was true and that a deep intuition and insight prompted me to speak to him in this way.

It felt daring and at the same time blatantly obvious.

This new mortgage proposal seemed all at once to be superficial and temporary to me.

It seemed like a continuum of my father's yearly gifts, a temporary fix to the money problems, but never a real solution.

I had a very deep sense that it would not help either our marriage or our finances in the long run and I refused to sign.

How I ever got the courage to stand up to him is beyond me.

There was the usual amount of rational persuasion, but maybe the fight wasn't in him anymore and after a while he seemed to accept that I couldn't be convinced to change my mind. I felt relieved that he hadn't tried harder.

But then something strange happened that I hadn't predicted or prepared myself for.

He switched off.

He shut down as literally as you might flick a switch when leaving a room to save on electricity.

He found some place inside that he accessed and then he turned it off. No more hugs, kisses, sex, conversation, shared discussions or intimacies. It was all over.

All gone.

Right then.

From then on.

We did talk about the kids, and the various schedules that

made up our lives, but that was it.

He started to not come home after work.

He didn't call, and he didn't explain himself when he did come home.

He started going into work later, taking longer lunches so he could get in a round of golf at Newport Country Club.

I felt shut out of his life, but also intuitively knew beyond a doubt that signing the loan application was not the answer.

I held my ground and watched as my marriage disintegrated.

24

Why do you weep? The source is within you. –Rumi

Feeling emotionally abandoned, I drew closer to my father who patiently listened and was smart enough to hold out on giving me any advice.

I had gotten my Real Estate license and was working at Carey, Richmond and Viking on Bellevue Avenue and he would stop in while he was out on his walks, going to the Redwood Library or the Reading Room. I would give him an update, but there weren't any changes.

Rob told me he wanted a divorce. He said I wasn't supportive of him, that I was selfish and self-centered, and not doing what was best for the family.

I asked for another chance.

I said I would change.

I was desperate and said I would do whatever it took to keep the marriage together. I had the impression that it was all up to me. I felt very alone and powerless.

The struggle began.

My friend, an attorney in Boston, said to me, –Fasten your seat belt, you're in for quite a ride.

She was right.

The legal proceedings were interminable, and the fees ran close to $20,000. My father kept track of everything in his *Line-A-Day* journal; my parents came to the courtroom as proceedings would invariably end in a continuance and the back and forth dance between counsel left us confused, exhausted, and angry.

Why did it have to take so long?

I lost count of how many continuances there were. Arguments about Rob's salary mainly.

In the last year he had finally started to make some money at the brokerage firm and his numbers didn't match mine. We had to fill out lengthy questionnaires that were part of the discovery the lawyers had given us. Why was he saying he made so much less?

He claimed he was making $12 an hour. He effectively reduced his income by about 75% and I was sure he had done it on purpose to manipulate the amount of child support he would have to pay.

I was naïve. I was anxious all the time. And I hated how the kids were dragged through it all. He disappeared, and we didn't know where he was for a month.

He had gone up to Rockport, was living with our old friend, Doug, and working for him at his painting business.

I felt betrayed and had to rely more and more on Daddy for both financial and emotional support. He began to pay the mortgage.

If everything could stay the same for the kids, I hoped there would be less pain. I wanted them to walk into familiar rooms, the toys lying on the floor as they had left them in the morning, rumpled clothes and covers untouched.

I couldn't face the idea of moving; being able to walk to their old school was so important to me. It was probably my own fear of change that wanted me to keep everything as it was. Everything was the same, but no husband and no father lived there anymore.

We had several sessions sitting around the dining room table with a family therapist who came to the house. Seth looked at the floor, Lilli looked at everyone with daggers in her eyes, and Jessica tried her very best to make everything all right.

I don't know if these sessions helped or not, but it was the right thing to do and I wanted to do the right thing. I was desperate to do the right thing. I wanted to fix them, mend the pain, and make it all go away. I wanted them to understand something I couldn't even understand myself. I wanted us to get through this with as little damage as possible.

–When you and Dad said you were getting a divorce, my heart broke and it will never mend, said Lilli.

How long does it take for a heart to mend?

I felt useless to them.

I floundered for a bit, still working at Real Estate, but when three sales fell through that first summer because of circumstances beyond my control, it became harder and harder for me to suit up and show up. I put on the right clothes, the high heels and panty hose, applying makeup that Mummy used to call *putting on my face* but my voice held no enthusiasm for cold calling or meeting with potential sellers or buyers. My picture on all my promotional material showed eyes that looked like a deer in the headlights.

A career that depends on commissions seemed so much harder than when I was married and mine was the supplemental income. I didn't think I had it in me, and I wasn't quite sure even was *it* was. I went back to teaching aerobics at a couple of studios, but again, my enthusiasm was waning and my smile felt phony. The motivating, upbeat former self was gone.

I got some jobs doing decorative painting which at least afforded me quiet and the time to get my work done. All my jobs came from friends who were trying to help me through this rough time and I was so grateful for them.

I felt the most comfortable at those times, the brush in my hand and the steps laid out before me. I had taken a course on Decorative Painting at Johnson's Paint Store in Boston and had loved learning the history and the different techniques.

Once again, the arts were there to buoy me up.

Some days I would dress up to go to the Real Estate office for a couple of hours, change into a leotard, tights and leg warmers for a noon class, then spend the afternoon working on a faux marble wall in a bathroom.

I knew that I was being resourceful and using all my talents and gifts, but it just left me feeling so scattered.

There's got to be a better way than this.

My car had all those things for each job stuffed together; the briefcase next to the aerobic bag, under the painting supplies, drop cloth included.

Maybe I'm going crazy I thought more than once.

I needed a plan. I needed a way to support us. I could only accept so much help from my dad, the child support was not reliable at that point, and I worried constantly about having to move, about further losses which I didn't really think I would be able to bear.

As I tried to keep things looking good on the outside, my insides were a tangle of fear, depression and anger.

My friends would agree with me; putting all the blame on Rob for the marriage ending. I just couldn't see how I could be responsible for any of the problems that we had.

After I told a friend how burned-out I felt from my odd

collection of jobs, I took their advice and called another friend whose husband owned a very successful restaurant down on Bowens Wharf, in the heart of Newport. She was happy to help and shortly after our conversation I began waitressing and started to put a plan together.

I would go back to school and take the general courses I needed, which weren't too many since I'd accumulated quite a few credits over the years. Then I'd apply to a new program that the community college had just started; an associate degree to be a Physical Therapist Assistant.

I thought if I could do that, I would have a real career. I was struggling with self-worth and would hear reports that my ex was telling the kids I wouldn't go far working as a waitress. Part of me didn't care what he said, but part of me still cringed at his criticism. Once I was accepted into the program, I found that there was still another hoop to go through.

I had never finished high school. Instead, I took courses from the International Correspondence School and I had earned a high school diploma through them.

I would wait for my thick study books to come and then wait to get the results of my tests. Doing that work made me feel like I had a purpose; I'm more than a high school dropout I could tell myself. I hadn't kept any record of it through the years, but my dad found a copy of the diploma in his files. The State of Rhode Island didn't want to accept it, so I had to take prep classes, then the GED itself.

My credentials weren't enough to satisfy the state, but I wanted to be in that program, so I had to play by their rules. I was going to do what I had to do. It felt humiliating to be going through it all, especially at my age. When the time came for the GED Graduation, I just had them mail the diploma to me. I had the highest score, but I still couldn't stand up among them and hold my head up.

The first semester at college had been a challenge; I hadn't been a full-time student for so many years. Keeping track of assignments due, getting all the reading done and trying to manage my time presented big challenges.

Without seeing it, I put my kids' needs aside as I worked, then took classes, then tried to study.

I made Hamburger Helper and ordered takeout pizza to put dinner on the table. We had grilled cheese and tomato soup night and pancake night and I tried not to think about how many vegetables they weren't eating.

I was obsessed with getting this done and when the stress mounted, I would overeat, then over exercise, then say that it wouldn't happen again.

The ongoing dialogue that flows between parent and child had stopped. I stopped knowing everything they were going through; too busy, too tired or worse, I wasn't there. Our neighborhood was so safe and quiet I thought they would be fine on their own, so I let them be alone while I went to work or went to school.

On Sundays, I would work a double, so they would be home alone from nine-thirty in the morning until ten at night. I made the most money by working weekends so that was what I did. I would check in with them by phone and cross my fingers there would be no fights, no trouble and they would be okay.

Sometimes it was okay, which meant to me noneventful. One night the police came to a large unsupervised party that was taking place while I was at the restaurant. Alcohol was found, all the kids were sent home, and I was called at work. I had to leave early to come home and the lost income pissed me off as much as the news from the police.

I just kept plodding along with blinders on as to how my children were doing.

My child is a reflection of how I'm doing.

Lilli was having a really hard time. I knew she needed more attention than she was getting, and she started acting out in ways not unlike mine when I was her age. The big difference was that I was sneaky and said whatever I thought my parents wanted to hear. Lilli seemed not to care about the consequences of her actions.

Trying to get close was futile, she kept pushing me away. As unmanageable as she was living with me, Rob thought that living with him would straighten her out. He was sure he would be able to bring her around and get her motivated to do better in school. I couldn't motivate her to do anything around the house; the minute she was home from school she would be in her room with the door locked.

I would knock and reason, I would bang and yell, I would pound and scream.

I had never experienced anything like this with anyone before. I couldn't find a way to connect with her.

She wanted nothing to do with her family and the screaming matches we had on a regular basis left me shaky and feeling beaten. She was running me out of the house and my efforts to make her behave were empty.

She did go to Florida to live with her dad, where he tossed her all black jeans and tees and bought her a wardrobe of aqua and peach happy clothes. She taped her poetry on the walls of her room and he took it down saying it was depressing. When she came back from Florida nothing had really changed and our relationship deteriorated further.

I couldn't handle her.

I should have got us both into family counseling.

I should have tried harder to get through to her.

She shut me out, I shut her out and our fights escalated.

Nothing changed but the passing of time.

One night she screamed at me,

—I know what you did. I know your secret.

—What are you talking about?

—I know you had two little girls and put them up for adoption. Dad told me what you did. You were incapable of love then and you still are. That's why you sent me to live with him. You couldn't handle me, so you sent me to Dad.

—When did he tell you this? Yes, it is true but it's not a secret. It's something I wanted to tell you when I thought you were old enough to understand. The timing just hasn't seemed right.

—He told me when I lived with him. He told me two years ago.

My heart stopped beating and I struggled to understand.

—You mean to tell me that you've known this about my past for two years and you've just kept it to yourself.

—Yes.

My heart started racing and I don't think I could have hated him more than in that moment.

It wasn't his business to tell her.

How on earth could a child begin to process this information? So much of her acting out now made sense to me but none of it could be undone. I just added it to my list of ways he had hurt me through hurting the kids. What could I do now?

Things did not improve between us for several years.

I felt I was failing at all my chances.

The funny thing about that kind of thinking is that it

totally circumvents the *day at a time* concept. The old thinking makes everything black and white, right or wrong. I'm a lousy parent or I'm a perfect parent and it's never been like that. I'm a human parent who just keeps trying to do better, to see more, feel more, and love more.

Every new day means I'm being given another chance.

25

The trouble is, you think you have time. —Buddha

The end was finally coming to the Physical Therapy program. One of my last clinical rotations was at a very busy outpatient clinic in East Providence. It gave me the chance to work with all kinds of rehab protocol and although people were there for a myriad of reasons, we often talked about all sorts of other things as their therapy took place.

A few patients had addiction issues in the past and we would discuss how using had left us bankrupt and almost killed us. How grateful we were for our lives today.

A mother overwhelmed with family demands and problems would find a willing ear in me as I worked on her tight upper trapezius muscles, manifested in part, by stress.

Life and all its many facets would often be discussed during these therapy sessions.

One woman with chronic pain had gruesome stories of loss upon loss. How she could bear all she had experienced was unfathomable until I realized that her body still held all the pain of her past. She wasn't free from it; it still bound her and held her hostage.

Unresolved grief can lead to emotional and physical problems that might not even seem related. I told her about being adopted as a baby and she urged me to begin a search. We talked about possible outcomes, and I knew that she was right but still, I took no action. It just seemed beyond my reach; something I thought would require all of me. I felt as thin and fragile as a new layer of ice, ready to crack through with the slightest pressure.

If I had found my birth mother then, how might that have changed things? I later learned that she had, in fact, died in 1978—the year between my having Jessica and the twins being born. She still would have been gone; any chance to meet her had evaporated. The past cannot be changed. I had to hit a bottom in my own soul before I became willing to do the work and to accept whatever might come out of it.

This was my life's work: to unravel and make peace with my past.

I would need to take responsibility for the breakdown of my marriage, to see how self-seeking had been the motivating force in my life and to become willing to make tangible changes. It wouldn't be enough to think about things, I would actually have to take some action.

Willingness would be the keystone to all lasting change.

I would have to ask for help to do all of this; I would have to admit that I could not do it alone. It would not be a matter of weakness in asking for help, it would be the start of finding strength.

In the process of excavation there would be pain that I would have to find the strength to face. I would come to realize that I was not alone.

I didn't have to go through everything alone.

My pride was going to be the death of me if I didn't do something different.

*

1/14/1993. *Sanibel-Captiva Islander* newspaper. Headline:
MAN KILLED CROSSING PERIWINKLE WAY AT COMMUNITY
CENTER.

My parents had been in Sanibel for only two weeks.

Once all their things were unpacked, Daddy set up his
portable Underwood typewriter on the kitchen table so that
he could keep up with his writing. He wrote articles for
Shipmate magazine and had co-authored *Sailors and Scholars:
The Centennial History of the U.S. Naval War College.*

Spending six weeks on the island was a perfect getaway
from the New England winter. There was a relaxed pace with
a minimum of social pressure and plenty of activities they
both enjoyed.

They walked the beach, ate at their favorite restaurants,
and had attended a lecture given by the Audubon Society that
evening. They loved going to those lectures—with a bird
book and binoculars always nearby, they were turning into
avid birders. They were chatting and walking hand in hand
as they stepped into the crosswalk that led to the parking lot
from the Community Center on Periwinkle Way.

They never saw the car coming.

It hit them both. It ended his life.

My sister called our house as soon as she had been
notified by the State Police, but I was still at work and Jessica
answered the phone. Marjorie told her to have me call as
soon as I got home but didn't say why.

It was a Sunday night in January and the restaurant was
quiet. Since I'd worked a double, they gave me the option to
get off early.

When I got home there was a note on the kitchen counter
that read: *Call Marjorie and please don't wake me up. xo Jessica*

Jessica knew that something was up, but it was a school night and she wanted to sleep, not worry.

I called Marjorie and she told me about the accident. She told me that Daddy had died and that Mummy was in Intensive Care. We weren't given much information about our mom's condition, but I had a deep sense of urgency. I told Marjorie I would make all the arrangements for us to get down to Sanibel.

Filled with pain and anxiety, I knew what I needed to do.

First things first. I immediately drove to the nearest gas station and bought a pack of cigarettes; I knew it would calm me down. I knew that smoking would ease the pain I was feeling so that I could do everything else.

I got home, ripped the plastic from the pack, and with shaking hands, lit the first cigarette I'd had in a few years. I didn't care about the consequences of smoking. I took the deepest drag I could. I then calmly started making the travel arrangements, booking the earliest flight for the next morning and reserving a rental car.

Next, I called my friend, Kathy, to see if Jessica, Seth and Lilli could stay with her family while I was gone, hoping she would be able to take them to school in the morning, pick them up, and have them sleep at her house. Before I had even finished asking she said, –Yes.

I went upstairs and looked in on my children and knew I would have to tell them soon, before I left. Letting them sleep as long as I could, I packed a small bag, including a bathing suit, which felt very inappropriate, but then, we were going to Florida.

The hours creeped by while I stared at the ceiling above my bed and smoked, trying to sleep, smoking more until it was time to get going. Marjorie would be waiting for me to drive us to the airport. Before I left the house that morning, still dark outside, I went in and woke each child and told them what had happened and what I had to do. I promised Kathy would take care of them and that I would call them right after they got home from school. I turned my face away after hugging them as my tears welled up.

–I can't start crying now, I told myself.

When we had a layover in DC, I called the hospital in Fort Myers and asked to be put through to Mummy's room, distractedly tapping my fingers against the metal shelf in the phone booth. It seemed to take forever to connect to anyone. Finally, I was speaking to the charge nurse who said Mummy had been asking for her husband. I told the nurse that we would be there soon and to stall off her questions until we got there.

–Please don't say anything to her, let me tell her.

We went directly from the airport to the hospital and quickly found her room, our anxiety building the closer we got to the inevitable.

Marjorie pushed me into the room first and we got our first look at Mummy lying in the bed; IV in her wrist, O2 line running to the wall behind her bed, a jumble of other lines and the monitor displaying her vital signs.

I looked at those numbers quickly and nothing I saw there made me panic more than just looking at her. She didn't look anything like herself with the head of the bed raised and legs elevated as both tibias had been fractured.

The swelling in her legs was grotesque and I looked back at her face. She looked like a withered grey bird lying among the smooth white hospital sheets, her feathers soft and wings broken.

Could this mess even be fixed? I thought to myself. Her

face ashen under the bandages, her eyes fluttered open when she heard our voices.

—We're here now, Mummy. Marjorie and I are both here.

—What about Jack? Where is your father? Her eyes bore into me. This isn't happening.

—You were both in an awful accident. Daddy didn't make it.

I wanted to say it in a way that wouldn't hurt. I didn't want to say it at all, but the words choked out of me.

She closed her eyes.

—It should have been me, she whispered.

I never in a million years would have thought this could have happened to our family. We all think we're so safe from tragedy; we don't live in a war zone or in a ghetto; these things happen to other people. These things happen in other places; a big city maybe, surely not on a street named Periwinkle Way. They were on the well-lit crosswalk for God's sake. It was an accident and accidents happen. This was an accident that couldn't be taken back; it was over in the worst kind of way with a loss of life that just didn't penetrate our brains.

It was more than a life; it was my Daddy.

That scene will be in my consciousness forever; sharply defining that moment in time. The next few days were a blur. Her twice than normal size legs had to be cut horizontally multiple times so that the fluid building up had somewhere to go.

Fasciotomy is a surgical procedure where the fascia is cut to relieve tension and pressure; without it the circulation is greatly impaired. The procedure can save the limb when the compartment syndrome is so advanced. The practice today of using pharmaceuticals to reduce edema wasn't used then, or maybe it wasn't working fast enough. All those cuts could set her up for more infection or worse, but that wasn't the primary concern at the time.

She stayed in Intensive Care while Marjorie and I walked on the beach on Sanibel Island and wondered aloud how beauty could still exist.

We saw a dolphin and were ashamed at our delight in watching its sleek form dive through the sparkle of Gulf waters, wondering if that one dolphin held our dad's spirit.

Where had he gone anyway?

We sat in the Jacuzzi by the pool and tried to not feel anything but hot water against our skin. We looked up at the stars and slept in the king-size bed our parents had slept in just two nights earlier, before the world had been set on its side.

The funeral home arrangements had to be made; we wanted to see his body but were not allowed.

–This is not how you will want to remember your father.

We pressed, and they let us be with him and we touched one cold blue foot.

–Yes, this is him, we nodded.

We looked at each other and shook our heads.

–No, this is not our father.

We got a little crazy waiting in the funeral home; laughing at nothing, but it all seemed so funny. We told each other to stop it; the funeral director could come through the door at any minute and find us behaving badly. We needed to pull ourselves together. We needed to grow up. We had to pick out an urn. We had to sign important papers. We felt completely helpless. How can a man who had survived the sinking of the *Yorktown* in WWII be killed crossing the street?

He was a hero, not the victim of a car accident.

Nothing seemed fair, nothing made sense and I couldn't forgive the driver of that car. I needed a good explanation. In the meantime, I smoked and made arrangements. Our father was cremated, and we flew back to Rhode Island. Mummy boarded the plane from an ambulance. She had a seizure the day before she was released; the first of many. Her injuries were multiple and complicated. But none of the losses could compare to losing her darling Jack. Immediately upon landing she was transported to Newport Hospital to begin a long period of rehab.

*

There was a memorial service at their church, Trinity, where he had volunteered as a guide once a week during the years they were in Newport.

It was held as soon as Mummy was thought strong enough by the hospital staff to attend. She was brought down by ambulance with an attendant, arriving in her wheelchair with her right leg straight out in front, the leg she almost lost, looking quite serene. She wore her mother's pearls and a dress that intensified the blue of her eyes.

I felt like it was all a dream; neither Marjorie nor I participated in that service.

We may have been in shock, letting others speak about our father. They paid heartfelt tribute to a man well loved and respected without emotion overtaking them. We sat up front with straight backs beside our mother and kept very still during the service.

The reception was a lovely blur, one after another person giving their condolences. There were so many people. He had reached so many people.

*

Years later I took my husband's shoes to the little shoe repair shop on Thames Street my dad often went to. The cobbler's name was George and his family had been repairing shoes at that location since 1947.

He had been in the Navy too—perhaps that was their bond but maybe it was something more.

Somehow my dad's name came up and he said:

—Ah, yes, the Admiral. What a fine man he was. Your father would always stop in when he was out for his walks and we would talk for a bit, whether he had shoes with him or not. He never acted like he was any different than me. He never held his rank over me. He always had a kind word for me. You take care of yourself now, George, 'til I see you again, he'd say to me.

My father walked every day; it was one of the things he loved the most about living in downtown Newport.

He would pay his bills in person, rather than mailing them off. He probably stopped often to chat with people as he did his errands.

Everyone loved my dad and had nothing but good things to say about him.

I never processed Daddy's death. If I allowed myself to feel that depth of pain, there would be no coming back. I was sure of that. The priorities were to somehow be there for my children, get back to work, and back to school. What was I going to do? Put my life on hold so I could process? No, I did my usual: push all the feelings down and act as if everything was fine.

26

Sorrow has its reward. It never leaves us where it found us.
                                              —Mary Baker Eddy

I went on autopilot after Daddy died. I stayed busy with family, the house, work, and a new semester of college. I cycled through these feeling numb most of the time. I wanted to be responsible and be a good example for my children. I didn't want anyone to know how I felt inside. I wanted especially for my children to think I was handling it. I was terrified of exposing them to my pain; it was too soon, I reasoned, after the divorce to have them go through any more. I was trying to protect them from life. Putting one foot in front of the other deluded me into thinking I was doing all right. The kids are healthy, the bills are paid, the house is relatively clean and there is food in the fridge. So what if I was depleted all of the time? Empty on the inside.

Insidious: proceeding in a gradual, subtle way, but with harmful effects.

I started going out after work with friends from the restaurant. I had a diet coke to their beer. We shot pool and I felt a little more relaxed, forgetting for a short time my real life. I started to hang at their house and after many times of saying, —No thanks, I said, —Here, let me have that.

I hadn't had a drink or a drug in seventeen years but one night I took a hit on a joint. Marijuana had never been a problem for me, I thought as I looked back. No blackouts, car accidents or anything remotely as crazy as other drugs and alcohol had been for me. I inhaled deeply, relaxed completely and thought to myself, I will only smoke on Friday nights.

Within a short time, it was daily.

Like slipping into the old jeans that are a little big, but so comfortable, the ones you never want to get rid of, I became a regular pot smoker. I never gave it a second thought. My grief management solution was to self-medicate and I thought it was working just fine.

I rationalized my habit, as I weeded the garden and prepared dinner for my kids. This isn't hurting anyone, I was sure. After all, it was natural, herbal, and helped me cope with my day-to-day life. As the weeks turned to months, I noticed I wanted to hurry home so I could smoke. I noticed how much I was looking forward to that part of my day. I noticed how I started to plan for when I could be alone and do my thing. At least I'm not drinking, I would think. Recovery was the furthest thing from my mind. I was so isolated from the people who had once been such a big part of my life; I wouldn't even know where to begin a conversation with any of them. I thought I could handle it.

Baffling: impossible to understand, perplexing.

I had forgotten everything that had at one time been ingrained in my thinking. It doesn't matter whether you drink it, smoke it, shoot it, snort it—it's all the same. If it alters your thinking, affects your consciousness, it's just not for you. Once an addict, always an addict. All of that knowledge drifted away in a cloud of smoke. I told myself I was different.

Smoking in the bathroom, blowing smoke out the

window so my children wouldn't know was a low point. My children were not enough to make me stop.

After graduating and getting licensed by the state, I returned to school to get a BS in Biology. My career and education were not enough to make me stop.

I would think I needed to get back to my tribe, to stop getting high, to get clean again, but I never took any action. My thoughts were not enough to make me stop.

Three years passed by, doing the same thing over and over.

One midsummer afternoon, my friend Leslie visited me, and I shared my concerns with her. It wasn't the first time she had patiently listened to me ramble on about what I needed to do to get my life back on track. I was feeling sorry for myself again, overworked and misunderstood. Like a broken record, I outlined the things I would do, and she paused before looking at me intently, and gently asking:

—Anne, what are you waiting for?

I had no answer. Never before had that question occurred to me.

After she left, I rolled a joint and took it out on my little bedroom balcony to smoke. The night was warm and the moon was shining its light into my gardens. I sat on the deck with my back against the house…and nothing happened.

I didn't get high.

Not even a little buzz.

Nothing.

Instead, I got a sense of impending doom like I had never experienced before. I would be arrested, lose my license, it would be in the newspaper, and I would bring shame to my mother and my children. All of the people and things so important to me now would be suddenly swept away.

The scenes of loss played through my mind like an old newsreel gone wildly off-track. I couldn't make it stop. I was full of fear and the night loomed ahead with no clear direction. My anxiety mounted as dawn approached. I couldn't get her question out of my head.

What are you waiting for?

Sleep never came, but the next day brought a feeling of decisiveness and clarity and with that, I made a plan. I went to where my old friends would be. I told them the truth and they welcomed me as if I had never been away. I felt like I had come home.

A simple question asked out of love, for which I had no answer.

This is how grace once again, entered my life.

I surrendered.

27

The beginning is always today. —Mary Shelley

I thought at first he wasn't my type.

I thought I was resolved to being single and it certainly couldn't be time for a relationship.

This one started as a simmer, totally unlike the rolling boils I usually leapt into.

This one made room for our differences and when he said, —We can agree to disagree, some forgotten longing opened in me.

Long walks turned to talks about childrearing. My youngest were twelve years older than his very young son who lived on the West Coast with his ex-wife.

We went for a visit and the child asked me:

—Do you love my Daddy?

—There are a lot of different kinds of love, I replied.

Then I went on to explain filial love, agape love, thinking it would all make sense to his six-year-old brain. Having both come out of painful divorces, we weren't rushing into saying the *L word*.

And so the courtship was slow, and thoughtful, and when Ted and I married three years later, it was with a deeper understanding and commitment than I had ever experienced before. Here was someone I could really trust, no matter what. A new way of relating, setting boundaries, thinking before I spewed out my emotional opinions and it gave way to a new kind of relationship. It was a new kind of love for me.

*

The kids were arriving home from a late summer vacation with their father and I headed to the airport to pick them up. The start of school was just a few days away. Only Jessica and Lilli were at the gate. Seth was going to be starting high school and Rob had decided that his opportunities would be better if he lived in Florida. His new wife had two younger sons from a previous marriage and he reasoned it would be perfect. They lived in a gated golf community and Rob could fulfill his dream for Seth to get a college scholarship for golf. They had played together since Seth was six and got his first set of clubs.

The girls told me that Rob hadn't called me because he knew that I wouldn't agree. He decided it was better to keep Seth there and deal with any repercussions later. When we did speak on the phone, Seth told me it was what he really wanted.

He wanted nothing more than to live with his father. He had never really talked about his feelings after the divorce, but I knew he adored and missed him and would do anything to please him. When they were together, they were inseparable, often walking hand in hand. Seth didn't care that he might be too old to hold hands, it was his Dad.

So that was that and the loss I felt was joined with all the other feelings of powerlessness and lack of control over anything that mattered to me.

Seth did come home for summer vacations and some of the other holidays. I would get so excited when I knew a visit was coming and we could all be together.

The Christmas before his senior year, Rob called the day before Seth was scheduled to fly home to say that he wouldn't be coming.

I was fuming but waited to hear the reason. I knew it was going to be some kind of bull. Rob thought it would be better if Seth concentrated on his school work as college application time was right around the corner and he hadn't done enough to warrant a vacation.

–This isn't a vacation!

–This is family time!

–We're all anxious to see him.

–His sisters have been talking nonstop about him.

–I've missed him so much, you're killing me on this one.

I didn't say any of that, but I was steaming inside. How could he do that? We already had the plane ticket.

The injustice of it was beyond my rational thinking but the conversation ended and there was nothing I could do. I sat down heavily on the bed and just couldn't hold back the tears. It was all just so unfair. I couldn't see Rob's side of it at all; maybe his reasons were valid but all I felt was a hurtful rage.

How could he do this to us?

Without even a discussion.

My resentments against my ex continued to grow; I rationalized them and felt that each one was justified. He had done the unforgivable: ending our marriage and hurting our kids. I couldn't think about him without seething. My friends were all in agreement, how can he do this to you?

When Seth finished high school, I had very mixed feelings

about going down to Florida for the graduation.

There was a part of me that didn't think I deserved to be there; the crazy part of my brain that wanted to keep me as the victim and sitting miserably on my old pity pot. Ted convinced me that I had every right to be there and share in his accomplishment.

We made the arrangements.

We got to Fort Myers and made our way across the sprawling campus of his high school to the huge auditorium where the ceremonies were being held. We found our seats and settled in; I was glad we had gotten there early. Before long, I spotted Rob, Jane and her two tow-headed boys filing in. She looked slim and pretty, her hair in a sleek up-do. I immediately started comparing and Ted had to talk me down.

–Relax.

I saw Seth walk the stage in that purple gown, taking too many pictures, but I didn't care; I was there and smiling nonstop, taking it all in. So many issues had come up for me around this graduation and I thought back to Jessica's high school graduation. Rob hadn't even made the effort to come. His absence was an unspoken mar on the day.

Afterwards, the parents and families flooded down to meet the new graduates. We pushed through laughing, happy groups to get to Seth. I reached out my hand to Rob and introduced him to my husband.

We said our hellos to Jane and her boys, and made some small talk. I glanced down and saw the black and white, two-tone wingtips Rob was wearing. At his neck, his preferred tie choice, the jaunty bowtie he had started wearing while we were still married. The man had lots of style, I had to give him that and in some circles, style can get you pretty far. I cared little for that kind of style anymore; I knew the superficiality of it and the constant need for more. When one want was met, another was soon created.

I had conquered some old fears about what I could do, where I could go and what I deserved. Seth had earned his diploma and I walked away with increased self-worth and a new confidence. I was remarried now and smiling happily on the arm of my husband. We said our goodbyes and that was the last time I saw Rob.

Ted and I rented a small powerboat the next day and got on the water with Seth, cruising the sound, enjoying the sun and each other's company. We shared a sense of accomplishment. Another chapter was about to begin.

*

I had decided to sell the big house in Jamestown that I had lived in with Rob, the house that our kids grew up in, the home where a dream began and sadly ended. With everyone moved on and out, it seemed pointless to stay. There were expensive renovations that we'd been putting off for years and my heart wasn't in it.

I had been staying at Ted's little condo in Newport, he had been staying with me in Jamestown, and it seemed like it was time to find a place of our own—with our new relationship, we wanted a fresh start.

When Mummy was discharged from the hospital she went to live with Marjorie. She still needed so much help with her daily activities. Therapy continued and several months later, she returned to the condo in Newport, but it soon became clear it was unsafe for her to live there alone. Too many stairs and too many memories. Once Daddy died, the attraction for her being in that condo diminished—nothing was the same without him. After much research and with a sinking inevitability we moved her into an assisted living facility where the common areas were decorated in blues and yellow.

—This will be a cheerful and appealing place for her to live, Marjorie and I said hopefully to each other.

Meanwhile the condo sat empty, with food still in the cupboards and Daddy's clothes untouched in the closets. The upper loft, which had been his haven, sat with dust gathering over his stamp collection and the photo-covered walls documenting his long and celebrated career in the Navy. It was too hot to really use that space in the summer, but the view was worth the three-flight climb.

Ted and I started talking about the renovations that we could do to the condo and make it our own.

We worked through the legalese so that it would be in my name. It was exciting to pick out materials and design our living space together. The tiny galley kitchen in the back of the condo became an alcove with a big new window overlooking the courtyard with weeping elm trees that attracted all kinds of song birds but screened out the shops and the people.

We moved the kitchen to the front of the condo, so we could sit at the massive granite counter and look out at Newport Harbor. A U-shaped banquette was built in a lost corner and we established a dining area. We had created an open floor plan and were enthusiastic with the results. I hoped that we could stay for a long time. The house in Jamestown was the longest I had ever lived anywhere, and I liked the idea of belonging to a place.

A sense of place that I'd never had growing up. A sense

of home that I had wanted so much for my children.

*

Everyone gathered with us in Newport for Christmas dinner. I looked around the room and felt so grateful for my family and for all the gifts that I had. I had been so devastated by my divorce and never imagined that things would turn out like this. I had married a remarkable man and my life was really beyond my wildest dreams.

We were stuffed on an overload of their favorite dishes and taking that welcome break between courses when the kids said they wanted to call their dad before the deserts were served.

Rob and his wife had separated and were in divorce proceedings, his house was getting ready to go on the market and he was at a low point. He had started drinking along the way, an innocuous rum punch on a cruise, and that sped up the end of his marriage.

After the phone had been passed around from Jessica, to Seth and then to Lilli, something in me stirred and I said that I wanted to talk to him too.

After months of prayer and writing about my part in our marriage, I was feeling less resentment towards him. It hadn't all been his fault. My heart had softened towards him as a man and a father.

–Please pass me the phone.

It wasn't a long conversation between us, we talked about our children and how well they were doing, acknowledging each other for our parts in helping them become the young people they were. And then I wished him well. I told him that I hoped that things would get better for him. I felt the animosity that had been between us for so many years dissolve. We wished each other a Happy New Year and said our goodbyes. That was the last time I talked to him. I had no idea that would be the case of course, and we were soon back gathered around the table. I had made a pumpkin pie, which had always been his favorite holiday desert.

*

Not long after our wedding, Ted got a call from his ex-sister-in-law that his ex-wife had had a relapse. She had been sober a number of years but we had no reason to keep tabs on her recovery. My husband was understandably upset, especially since we were in Rhode Island and she and their son, Alex, lived in Santa Barbara.

–Let's go get him, I said.

My instinct was to bring Alex home with us while his mother was getting clean again. I didn't think or hesitate for a moment. I realized later how much healing had taken place within me; I hadn't thought of myself first. I knew intuitively what the right thing to do was, and I was ready to do it.

I was putting someone else ahead of me.

Another sign that I was growing up.

The time in Santa Barbara was painful for everyone. Ruth came by to say goodbye and Alex clung to her and sobbed and would not let go. She had to push him off and left so quickly we all shuddered with feelings of being ripped open. We hoped to God we were doing the right thing.

The first few weeks he was with us were even more difficult; he cried every night for her and there was no consoling him.

Both his Dad and I wanted him to see how it was for the

best that he was with us but try explaining that to a nine-year-old.

—You're going to be okay.

—It's going to be okay.

Easy words for an adult to say.

Ted took him to church and Alex asked the congregation to pray for his mother. They went to a different church every week hoping something would click for Alex, but it didn't. Eventually they stopped going and we introduced him to journaling.

—Just try to write down how you feel. No one will read it and maybe it will help you feel better.

We talked to him about living one day at a time. He gave us a wan smile.

We found a therapist and Alex made weekly visits, but the shell protecting him wasn't ready to crack.

Alex stayed with us for the rest of the year and through the summer but went back to his mother for the beginning of the next school year. She was ready to take him, and he couldn't stand the thought of being away from her any longer.

It had been a hard year. Alex needed constant help with his homework. He was having trouble comprehending what he read, so we sat together and took it all line by line, subject by subject. I never expected to be performing this parental task again, but in the face of what he needed, I wanted to there for him.

I could see how the universe was giving me another chance to be a parent.

He was heartbroken, and I knew as much as I gave him time and love, I wasn't his mother.

He still cried himself to sleep.

I fell into bed each night exhausted.

We met with his teachers and everyone thought it would be best if he repeated the grade—much had been lost because the move to Rhode Island had been so traumatic for him. He sure didn't want to do that, so he went in at the next grade level home in Santa Barbara only to be moved back a grade before Columbus Day.

I wish I could have done more for him.

Oh, how not to have regrets for what has happened.

If only I had done this, or maybe that.

Yet I know I did the best I could.

28

Everything you want is on the other side of fear. –Jack Canfield

The universe has no timetable, no punch in clock that says:

–Too late for you. The opportunity has passed.

There is no limit to when we can find redemption and see the world and our circumstances in a new light.

I thought that I would always think a certain way about my life.

What had happened. The choices I had made.

I didn't think there could ever be a different way to look at things. I didn't think a complete healing of my heart could ever occur.

The damage I had done could never be righted and I would just have to learn to forget about it.

In my limited thinking, letting go and trying to forget about it were indistinguishable.

*

The light was fading as I read the local free weekly paper and came across an item that made me catch my breath.

The room felt completely silent, as if waiting to see what my reaction would be. I watched the dust motes float in the late afternoon light.

TONIGHT: READING AND TALK BY ANN FESSLER, AUTHOR WHO CHRONICLED ONE HUNDRED STORIES ABOUT GIRLS GIVING UP THEIR BABIES FOR ADOPTION PRE-ROE VS WADE.

The Girls Who Went Away was published in 2006 and my story could have been among them. Many girls had been sent away by families who couldn't stand the shame their daughter's condition would bring upon them. It was also my mother's story, but I didn't know that yet.

I hadn't considered my family at all when I found myself pregnant at sixteen. Being pregnant seemed like an answer to all my problems. We could just get married, be on our own, and life would be wonderful. Naïve, self-deluded and wrong about every aspect of my decision.

What could I possibly learn from this author, who had been adopted herself? I was a woman who had also been adopted as a baby and ended up surrendering two children. But with a growing urgency and unrest, I went to the Newport Public Library to hear what she had to say.

On the one hand, I was overwhelmed with feelings of relief that this subject was being so openly discussed, but the room was too bright—I felt strangely exposed. And everyone there seemed to be with someone else; why had I come alone?

I could feel my anxiety growing.

I wanted to say something. I wanted to disappear. I wanted her understanding and her compassion. I wanted to run out of the room. Who did I think I was trying to go back into the past, looking for forgiveness and some kind of peace? But I did put my hand up, told a brief edited story, saying I had given up one child, not two. Surely that would put me into another category.

When the talk was over, I went up to the author and admitted my lie.

–There were two, I whispered.

I had to tell the truth even though I was sure she would be filled with disgust. But we talked, and she gave me the response I needed to hear.

Don't wait.

Start now.

Look for them.

You won't regret it.

I wanted to believe her, but I was filled with fear.

I went home flipping through her book, looking for the passage that would be my answer. Always and still looking outside of myself to find answers to what could only be found by going inward.

*

I lay tossing and turning, unable to get my brain to quiet down enough to get to sleep. I thought of something else I had read once about not regretting the past or wanting to shut the door on it. That couldn't be accurate I thought; I've remembered it wrong.

How can someone who has done what I've done, not regret the past?

Unthinkable.

How could I not wish it away, push all thoughts of it down, be filled with remorse whenever I thought of my regrettable actions?

I wanted to forgive myself, but I just couldn't seem to do it. There had to be something that I was missing. I had brief feelings of forgiving myself, but it never lasted.

I felt like I was trapped in a maze and there was no way out. I got up, fumbled for the light, found the book, found the passage, and sighed deeply.

I had remembered it correctly. I went back to bed, still uneasy, still restless, still longing for relief.

How could I not regret the past?

I simply could not forgive myself for what I had done.

Maybe a miracle like that could happen in someone else's life, but not in mine. Not yet.

*

I had learned to meditate. But sometimes, when I quieted down enough, memories flooded my consciousness and I couldn't let go of them. I felt the old sadness well up in me and I knew the tears would start to flow.

I felt completely alone with no one who could help. I felt as small and without any more substance than a speck of dust.

Where is God in all of this?

But eventually through meditation, I learned to call on the universe, all the good in the universe, all the love I could imagine, all the light and angels and forces for good to come to me, to be in my heart, to change my thinking.

I felt if only I could open my heart enough, I could be healed.

I called upon the highest power for good to heal me.

And then it happened.

I felt a shift inside.

A subtle, but substantial shift occurred.

The plug that had stopped up the drain for so long had

been pulled and there was a flowing sense of good that I could feel in my body. It was not some imagined sensation, but an actual warmth and sense of things being all right.

The tears stopped as easily as they had begun and I knew that the shift had been real, it was something that I could begin to build on.

If I had known it would take as long as it did to come to the truth about my past, and the miracle of finding strength and courage to put my deepest wishes into action, I surely would have started sooner.

But would I have?

Doesn't everything happen at the right time? More trust and more acceptance is always what I need. I have only been able to proceed falteringly, slowly, and with many stops along the way.

I lack courage, I lack perseverance.

Yet the facts are this: I *have* courage and I *have* persevered. It just didn't always feel that way.

And when I finally stopped judging myself, the light shone in through that crack.

29

There is a crack in everything, that's how the light gets in.
—Leonard Cohen

Soft April morning light was starting to fill the bedroom as I stood by the window. The phone rang, but when I answered it all I could hear was ragged breathing.

Then I realized it was my daughter, Jessica. She was hysterical, her voice barely intelligible.

—Jessica, slow down, I can't understand you.

—Dad's dead.

It didn't make sense to me. I knew my dad was dead, why was she telling me this?

—Not your dad, Mom. *Our* dad is dead.

I sat down on the edge of the bed. I took a breath even though my heart had started to pound. I know how this feels—Oh God, and now it's happening to her.

I later read the police report through tears that wouldn't stop.

Rob was in an accident on his motorcycle.

He was with his new girlfriend, Mia, and they had been drinking at a Harley Davidson clubhouse in Fort Myers. They had been there all afternoon and when they left, he was driving so erratically that a motorist called the police to report him.

They came too fast over the crest of a hill with a blind

view. They didn't see the semi-trailer truck that was making an illegal turn on the road ahead.

The Harley crashed into it and Rob and Mia were killed instantly.

That day eight children lost their parents to drunk driving. His three with me, his two young stepsons, and Mia's three.

I made the arrangements for Jessica, Lilli and me to go down to Fort Myers for the funeral. Seth flew in from San Francisco and we clung to each other for comfort.

We met Rob's family; the family that had blamed me for the breakdown of the marriage. At the time they had taken sides with their son and I was immediately left out in the cold.

When I saw his mother, my body started to involuntarily shake; an unpredicted sensation. We picked up the pace as we got nearer and hugged each other.

—Anne, you were always good to me. I'm so sorry I shut you out when you and Rob divorced, she said. —I felt like I had to stand behind him. I felt like I had to take sides.

—All that is behind us now, I said as I held her close.

An old friend of ours at the funeral told me that Rob was trying to get his life back on track.

This was the man that Rob had gone to live with when our marriage ended.

I'm sure they had many talks about how I had ruined everything and how it was my entire fault, but maybe he only listened and let Rob rant. Maybe he just let him get out all that anger.

At times, I had felt like he knew my husband better than I did, but now we connected, feeling a shared loss. Maybe our hurt had different origins, but it didn't matter.

He told me that Rob was determined to get sober again,

as soon as his house sold and a few other things were taken care of.

—I will get my shit together once I get my ducks in a row.

I looked around at all the people who had been part of his life; devastated by this untimely tragedy.

Rob's estranged wife was there with her two boys by her side, their blonde hair plastered down. These were the children from her first marriage to another alcoholic.

Rob had had a new family, but in the end, family can't keep you or your life together if you're an alcoholic who keeps on drinking. Divorce proceedings were underway, and they had been separated for a few months.

I knew there were three things that can happen to an alcoholic who doesn't stop drinking. Jail, institutions, or death. Rob continued to drink, in spite of not wanting to, and here we were at his funeral. We called it a celebration of his life.

After people spoke, we were invited to share, and Seth went up to the front and began to sing *The Time Warp*. His tentative voice was small and shaky to start but gained in confidence as anyone who knew the lyrics joined in.

It's just a jump to the left and then a step to the right.

The Rocky Horror Picture show had been a family favorite. Maybe it's not a film for kids but mine knew all the words to all the songs, and it was a uniquely perfect moment to hold Rob up with a memory of the good times. We sat together, clasping each other's hands and singing with tears streaming down our cheeks.

Lilli's best friend had been given the black and white wing tip shoes that Rob wore at Seth's graduation. I thought how well they went with her white double-breasted suit.

Later we went to Rob's sister's house and ate too much

and those who drank, drank, and he was remembered with funny stories.

Our good intentions made us promise to stay in touch.

*

Within a few days, depression set in. The same kind of suffocating lethargy I had felt after Daddy was killed in that accident. Bright colors were dull, my tongue insensitive to the taste of food. Did it matter if I hadn't washed my hair? I had to force myself to get out of bed and get going with the day.

In a way, it took me off guard because our divorce had been uncompromisingly painful. I had dwelled for so long on the many reprehensible acts he had committed. The sadness felt ancient and deep.

Back in therapy we talked about how all the deaths in a person's life are related and when someone close dies, memories of all the other deaths resurface. I was afraid of that.

So, I had to grieve my father and really process my feelings. I couldn't skirt around the pain anymore.

Then I got in touch with how much I had loved Rob. I grieved the loss of our marriage and all the plans we had made.

I cried over his humor and strength and that big huge smile. I remembered everything that had been good between us and let myself feel each moment. I imagined him as a little child, before living changed perfection. I grieved my children's loss and felt their suffering threefold.

*

Something shifted in me again and I didn't want to stay shut down any more. I didn't want to keep the hurts stuffed inside. If I really wanted to get better, I had to learn how to let go.

I'm interested in what happens during the rest stops, how things that were unclear become clear, how fears melt away. When my heart is open, it may be the moment when grace enters.

When I feel overcome with inertia, I have trained myself to sometimes not think, not let my conscious mind play with the idea of outcome and all the possible what ifs, and just move forward into action. Do the next right thing.

In the beginning of recovery there is always a lot of talk about action.

Overly analytical thinking and being stuck inside our heads is not healthy for most alcoholics. Like going to a bad neighborhood, it can be dangerous. One negative thought attracting another like a powerful magnet.

The action doesn't have to be dramatic; it can be as simple as pushing the covers back and putting my feet upon the floor and stepping outside for a walk. It can be as simple as looking up a phone number and making a call. Small actions count.

I thought: If not now, when?

I was ready to look for my daughters.

30

Are you willing to be sponged out, erased, cancelled, made nothing? Are you willing to be made nothing? Dipped into oblivion? If not, you will never really change. –DH Lawrence

Once again, I had started working with my therapist to specifically address all the issues that could surround a search. I thought I wanted to approach it in a methodical manner, not to be too emotionally attached to it all.

What was I thinking?

She put it to me in her gentle way.

How could I ever be in the right frame of mind unless I felt all the emotion again, to uncover all the feelings that went with that time?

Every session brought me to tears. I kept the tissue box close by. The moist clumps softly dropped into the waste-paper basket when I got up from the couch.

Every session brought me closer to the confused, isolated, and fearful girl that I was. The teenager who was trying hard to play grown up but hadn't any of the skills to make it work. It was almost inevitable that things would turn out the way that they did, and I began to get a sense that I *had* made the right decision.

I had done the best that I could with what I had to work with at the time. I started to believe a new truth about myself. I wasn't the worst girl alive, or any of the other derogatory names I so often called myself.

Addiction had been directing me all the time. I thought the problem was that I had married too early, to the wrong man, had kids before I could be a good parent, and on and on.

The truth was that I was an addict and that all my decisions were drug affected. The big and the small decisions were alike.

I needed to let go of my old way of thinking and take a real leap of faith.

*

My first attempt to find my daughters occurred when I visited my cousin for Easter with the kids after Rob and I had divorced in 1989. As our children played, we talked. In a spurt of bravery, I called and requested the forms I needed to put my name on a registry.

I still have the forms from Adoptees-In-Search, Inc. The envelope is dated 1990. If my daughters ever did a search for me, I would be easier to find. My name had changed so many times, with each relationship either adding or dropping a name. Putting all those names down could make it more likely for them to locate me.

Still thinking I could take a passive role, I again did nothing but drop the envelope into the adoption file I kept in my desk. Maybe one day I could fill it out and send it off.

*

My therapist said that I had to find my birth mother before I started a search for my daughters. She said it was part of the process and would give me a better perspective.

I trusted her but at the same time, I wanted to skip that part. I hadn't had much interest in my birth mother before. I had never thought of her as a real person. I never wondered what was going on in her life when she gave me up. I had never put myself in her shoes.

It was time for me to feel what it was like to be unplanned, unwanted and considered a burden.

I never thought of myself as being a problem in someone's life in that way. I had never considered that I wasn't wanted before. I had been told I was the *chosen baby* for so long that I only thought of my adoptive parents and me. I hadn't thought of the girl who had me and then gave me up.

*

She had gone away—been sent away—by her family, to live with her older married sister until I was born and then given up. Maybe then she could get her life back. Exploring all of those feelings was painfully insightful. It gave me time to think about what she must have been going through, especially the helplessness of having someone else decide what was going to happen to your child. She didn't have any say in the matter. She was a teenager just like I had been, and all the power was in the hands of her parents.

–We're doing this for your own good. You'll thank us later. You'll see, it's for the best.

I had always felt too uncomfortable to broach the subject of finding my birth mother with my parents, as if asking would make me seem somehow ungrateful and unloving. After Daddy died, I did talk to my mother about wanting to search for my biological mother. We went out for coffee and sat by a window that streamed winter light onto our table.

We gazed into our cappuccinos. Anxious to hear her response, grateful to hear, –You have my blessing.

She was as supportive and loving as the rest of my family had been.

She said, –I may have heard that they ended up getting married, your birth parents.

And my sister said, –You can't have too much family.

*

I still had the other forms I had sent for years before tucked into the adoption file I rarely looked at. The forms are blank and the postmark from the Rockingham County Probate Court date from the spring of 1997.

It had involved writing a letter to a judge who would then decide if the case was worth looking into. I tried to think of what I could say. I wrote a letter.

To whom it may concern:

Do I even have a right to know my own heritage? Is there a genetic tendency to seek blood kin as birds have homing instincts? I believe that hard wired into my genetic makeup is an instinctual drive to know where I came from. There is the huge aspect of absent and unknown medical history, which could be useful for my own health care or to give to my three children. Being chosen was a passive experience and my birth story was always a positive one, but as I grow older, I would like to know the true story behind the fiction I was told as a little girl.

I am finally prepared to know the truth about my past, with no expectations of any kind. My family tree is a fictional hoax, albeit a very respected and admired one. I am grateful for all the opportunities and privileges I was given by my parents, who are my family and who I deeply love. But it is not about loving them or loving them less because they withheld the truth from me. It is about wanting to know the truth about my genealogy, who I came from, the authenticity of my existence, not the adopted version.

I feel like I have been living one life, but there is another layer of who I am, my blood family, that I want to know the truth about. I feel as if I were to not pursue this search, I would be shutting the door on myself. I do not attempt to change the past, I accept all the choices that were made in my best interests, but the time has come to be fearless and responsible and seek another level of truth and consciousness.

The cultural norm in our society is to know who our parents are and deprived of this information my personality and psychological development were undeniably affected, especially during my teens and early twenties as I searched for the meaning to my life. Those were difficult years. Thankfully I have matured and gained wisdom and insights about myself. But there still exists many unanswered questions that can only hope to be answered by knowing the truth.

Open the files and grant me access to this personal information.

I never mailed the letter.

And why not?

No one person was going to hold my fate in their hands. Hands I was sure would not look at me with any heart or understanding. And so I did nothing; another rest stop along the way. I couldn't handle the thought of being rejected and judged again. I couldn't take that kind of chance. It was easier to do nothing.

The years went by.

31

Leap and the net will appear. —John Burroughs

The records in New Hampshire, where I was born, had just been opened and the procedure to find a birth parent had changed completely. It was no longer a process that involved a single judge determining my fate. Marjorie had seen an article dated January 6, 2005 from the *Concord Monitor,* and excitedly told me about it.

The bill had been sponsored by Senator Lou D'Allesandro who had himself adopted a daughter whose adult medical problems brought to light the importance of adoptees having access to medical history information. He proposed a new law to give adult adoptees the answers to which they are entitled and which the rest of the population has always had.

The door that had been closed for so long was beginning to open and my anticipation mounted.

That night was a restless one. I tossed and turned, deeply aware that the course of events would be beginning to change.

The next morning, I called the number for the New Hampshire Division for Children, Youth and Families, finally speaking to someone that could help.

They told me I would be getting a letter, but it could take some time before the process would get started. The letter eventually came, and I was assigned a case worker who was helpful during the waiting process and well as throughout the search process. They sent me an application for a copy of a non-certified, pre-adoption birth record. By May of 2006 I received a letter granting the release of my original birth certificate.

Her name was Marilyn and she was sixteen when she gave birth to me. My case worker also got me a copy of her death certificate and her obituary.

My hopes of her being alive were smashed and yet another loss was felt. Her parents were Irish, married and both twenty-five years old when they had her, their third daughter. I got a copy of the adoption form she and her mother had signed with my parents' signatures above. She later married the man who had been her boyfriend at the time she got pregnant and they later had two other children. Gary was born in 1951 and Nanci in 1955.

Marilyn died of breast cancer in 1978. She was forty-five years old. That was the year I was pregnant with Seth and Lilli. Jessica was a precocious early walker and my hands and heart were full.

My social worker helped me contact Gary and Nanci.

I gave her regular updates about the contact in an exchange of emails:

Gary and I have been emailing and it's been good. He told me he's taking it slow with his Aunt B—Marilyn's sister—but that he emailed her my picture. She wanted to see what I look like. Nanci has sent me two stacks of photos that are amazing. She had been told that Marilyn became pregnant after an attack by a drunk neighbor while babysitting. She went to live with her married sister in Portsmouth, where she had me. B's husband told Nanci that Marilyn got drunk and got pregnant, so their stories are conflicted. Which story is true? Gary and Nanci don't talk much so I don't want to tell Gary what Nanci told me. It's all very complicated and sad. I think they have a few issues between them, ah, family stuff. Something happened when their Dad died. Nanci told me she was sure that Victor and Marilyn were dating when the pregnancy occurred, so he did right by marrying her, after she gave me up for adoption. I'm afraid I might not find out the truth. My husband is more overwhelmed than I am, so many new people to consider.

My social worker wrote back:

I'm curious if you look like either Gary or Nanci. I know you've had a lot to take in over the last few days, try to be patient with yourself. It is mind boggling and sometimes even though questions are answered, those answers lead to more questions. It will be quite a process for you. Please take your time with everything and don't be afraid to set boundaries. I did talk with Gary about your Aunt. He really feels that it would be best for him to talk with her, as she is older and a very private person. He thinks that she would act like she knew nothing if I contacted her. I feel that we have to trust his judgment on this as he knows her quite well. Let's hope that she is open, it would fill in quite a few gaps for you. Please let me know if there is anything else I can do for you. I hope this journey has been worth the effort.

The first time Nanci and I talked, I took a page of notes, not wanting to forget anything she told me about my birth mother.

She also told me about herself. She had got pregnant when she was fifteen and her parents raised her daughter for her first three years when she was having problems with alcohol and drugs herself.

She said that her father had been physically and verbally

abusive to them, she described him as a domineering and demanding husband who had many extramarital affairs.

His advice to her had been to get married and get a job. Marilyn had been addicted to prescription drugs to lose weight and calm down and had, at one low point, tried to commit suicide. They lived with their paternal grandmother, who was from Poland, a very strict old-world Catholic in a house in town. When summers came, they went to a lake cottage and the grandmother stayed in the town house.

Nanci said that was when her mother was the happiest and most carefree—those summers out at the lake. Nanci was very angry that this big secret—that she had a sister—had been kept from her.

*

I did a painting on the day I found out that Marilyn had died. A small still life—a seashell on my desk with a view to the garden behind. A small painting in gouache in my art journal. A strange sadness, a loss for someone I had never known.

Shortly after the first phone conversation with Nanci, she sent me a little photobook with pictures of Marilyn, as a girl, with her sisters, with her husband, as a child and as an adult. I looked for the resemblances and saw the dimple in her chin.

I searched her face for more clues to see her personality, to hear the sound of her voice. The old images had nothing more to say even as I stared and stared.

*

The people in my birth mother's life who were older and in control used that control and changed the course of her life. They changed the course of my life too.

They did what they thought was the best thing to do. They did what they thought was right for their daughter. They did what they thought was right for the family.

Marilyn never told her story to her children, not even when she took care of her granddaughter for three years. She didn't want the courts to take the baby away because of Nanci's drug use.

She kept her secret about me from everyone.

*

Nanci sent me a beautiful card and inside she wrote:

Dear Anne

Some of the information you and I have learned about the past, the secrets and lies have been very hard to hear and to accept. But we are never given more than we can handle. I am so grateful to be an addict so that I have the tools of the program available to me that will enable me to get through this. I've heard through enough recovery talk from you to know you are in the same place. So, with this sadness comes the greatest gift. I (and you) have a sister! I feel so lucky. Just with the little bit we've talked, I think we have so much in common and I really look forward to this journey. I hope you do too. I will pray every day for both of us for acceptance of the past knowing that nothing can be changed and all involved were only human doing the best they can with what they have. God bless you Anne (and me) and our future. Love, Nanci

I've heard you're as sick as your secrets and I believe it.

A secret can't exist without some sort of story to hold it up, like poles for a tent.

When one pole goes, the rest are in danger of pulling the

tent down. The stories around a secret are really lies.
  If I confess to that, you might not like me.
  If I admit to this, you might judge me
  I just didn't dare to take that kind of risk.
  Until finally, one day, I wanted to be true to myself.

32

May I have the courage today
To live the life that I would love
To postpone my dream no longer
But do at last what I came here for
And waste my heart on fear no more. –John O'Donohue

I met Nanci at a Whole Foods on Route 495 that was half way between our homes.

I got there before she did and took a booth by the window so that I had a good view of the parking lot. I knew it was her as soon as she came into view. She was carrying heavy photo albums and had an expectant look on her face.

She made her way toward me. We greeted, hugging first, and then standing at arm's length so that we could see each other. We both had brown eyes and a dimple in our chins but that's where the similarities stopped.

She was six years younger than me but didn't look it.

She hadn't been able to take good care of herself and it showed. Addicts can have bad teeth and hers showed years of neglect. I watched myself forming opinions of her and told myself to stop it. Life had been hard for her but as we talked about our childhood and our early drug and alcohol use the similarities were more obvious than the differences.

It took a long time before we could settle down enough to get something to eat.

We looked at the albums together and her life played out in front of me, from the sweet child to the teenager with an attitude.

She showed me pictures of herself as a young mother and pictures on the couch with a cigarette in one hand and a drink in the other. Photographs can tell so much about people and their relationships; just from body language. How close people sit, whether that smile looks sincere, where people put their hands in relation to the other people. We shared many stories about our lives, but it wasn't until it was almost time to say goodbye that she told me that she was gay. I'm not sure why she waited so long to tell me, but it didn't matter to me and I told her that.

–I'm just happy that you found someone you love and who loves you back. Isn't that what we all want anyway?

Maybe she hadn't been accepted by people who mattered to her.

That meeting ended and I still hadn't told her about my daughters. Maybe I thought that might be too much for her to handle. Maybe I felt that she might judge me. I kept my secret.

*

It wasn't until the next time we met; maybe a year or so later that I did get completely honest with Nanci. We met at a Starbucks in Newburyport and I noticed how much thinner she was. She told me she had colon cancer and it had progressed and she had gone through all the available treatments and there was nothing more they could do. She said that she was on Palliative Care now and was feeling pretty good.

She had lost so much weight since the last time I had seen

her; all her curves gone, whittled down by the disease. I noticed how high her cheekbones were. We walked to a seafood restaurant on the docks and sat on an enclosed deck and ate clam chowder and clam cakes. I told her I had given up my two daughters when I was nineteen. She listened and did not judge me, and it reminded me that so much of what's going on, is just in my own head.

She reached for my hand across the table.

—We both went through a lot of shit when we were using.

Nanci and I understood each other. We were both addicts and had known loss. She had a daughter whom she had been estranged from for years. Even dying, there would be no reconciliation.

—Look how good you are doing now, she said to me.

All at once I felt so terribly sad. I was sad her life had been so painful and now she was dying and there was no way anyone would change the end of her story. She hadn't had the kind of success in her life that you could measure by worldly standards. Her car was late model, and her home was a trailer that needed roof repair with an old blue tarp taped to her bedroom ceiling. She shared about the strong support system she had with other women in recovery and how grateful she was to them. She was grateful too, that I had reached out to her. I was her only sister and she was so happy to know she had a sister.

—I always wanted a sister, she said.

*

The next time I saw Nanci it almost didn't happen.

Gary called me and told me he thought I should know that Nanci was on hospice care and didn't have long to live.

Her son had moved in to take care of her and Gary had been down to visit. He said it didn't look good. He meant she didn't look good. I said I had called but hadn't heard back from her and wondered what was going on. I had tried to email her too, but nothing there either.

–I'd like to see her.

–That wouldn't be a good idea, Gary replied.

I wanted to know why, and he just said it was a pretty depressing scene. I asked him if Nanci's son knew about me. He said he did know that she has a sister that was given up for adoption as an infant and they had been recently reunited.

That was a huge relief because if he had no knowledge of me, I would have to handle it another way. I didn't think it would be fair to lay all that on him now, when his mother was dying. I wanted to see her, but I was really more concerned for how he was doing. I asked for his phone number. I wanted it to be his and Nanci's decision.

Gary had been to see his sister, made his peace, but now it was my turn. If only they were willing. I sent up a silent prayer that I would not be too late.

–I'm going to call him and see what he thinks about me coming up to visit Nanci.

One last time. I don't want her to die without a chance to say goodbye. Gary didn't argue, he understood what I needed to do.

I called Derek right after I hung up with Gary and after a moment of awkwardness, he sounded very glad to hear my voice. I was the aunt he had heard about but never met.

–I'm thinking about driving up for the day to see your mom. Do you think that would be okay with her? Would it be okay with you?

He answered, Yes, without a moment's hesitation. The next day was Saturday and I said I would plan to get there before lunch. I wrote down the address and he gave me directions.

I was both excited and nervous on the drive up to Portsmouth, New Hampshire to see them. I wanted to be there for Derek, if only for a few hours, in what would be one of the most challenging times of his life.

I didn't know what to expect so I kept thinking about the most positive and loving attitude I could bring to the situation. I knew that I didn't want to be overly-caring and fussing; Nanci wouldn't have gone for that—she was a pretty pragmatic person from what I knew of her.

I knew so little about her really, but I was an addict too.

That gave me an insight to her illness and her state of mind that I hoped would help me. It was the kind of situation I used to run from; pain of any kind had to be avoided, yet here I was, driving straight for it. I felt like my heart was open.

Thank you, God.

Since it was Saturday there wasn't the usual bog of traffic and I got through Boston easily and then onto 95N into New Hampshire. It was a warm summer day and most of the traffic was headed to the coast. I was glad that I had gotten an early start. After talking with Derek, I couldn't tell how much time Nanci had left and I felt an urgency to get there.

I thought about how Nanci had told me she had never really left her birthplace; how very different it had been for me.

I had lived in three different states and a foreign country by the time I was ten. Traveling with my family had allowed me to see so much and had really given me a broader perspective on the world; I felt privileged on many levels as my life experience had been enriched.

It happened without even leaving home when we gathered in Jamestown and watched my grandmother's home movies of her African adventures. She had gone on safari multiple times, ever watchful with her camera, not wanting to miss anything. I thought of my grandmother as I drove; I didn't want to miss this experience either.

I was calm until I got to Nanci's street and saw one tired rundown trailer after another. I remember how Gary had told me she had inherited their parents' house in town but had sold it when times got tough.

My heart ached for the impulsive decisions made when we are in the thick of our addiction. Those decisions seem so right at the time and then we are stuck living with the consequences. I don't know what kind of house she grew up in, but I guessed it was much nicer than where she lived now.

Kids' bikes were left upturned, old charcoal grills and rusty lawn chairs, along with Rubbermaid sheds and all the extra stuff that people accumulate when their possessions outgrow their living space. Everywhere I looked I saw broken down old appliances and big black plastic bags.

Derek greeted me at the door with a big, warm hug and invited me in right away. He had a sweet face and beautiful eyes and I could see that he was glad I was there. He told me that the hospice nurse had been there the day before, but she wouldn't be back until Monday.

He sounded a little lost—he had no idea of what the weekend would bring. Nanci was lying on the edge of her queen-sized bed with a commode close by. She had been able to walk to the bathroom until just the previous night, but things had changed rapidly.

She had also been able to sit up but was much weaker now. When Derek tried to get her to sit up, she just fell heavily back to the pillow.

She looked so tiny in the bed; she had lost even more weight since I had seen her. Her face was drawn tight and her skin had no warmth or color. I got close to her and said:

—Hey, Nanci, it's Anne, your sister. I wanted to come and see you. I'm glad I'm getting a chance to meet Derek too. It's so good that he's here now to take care of you.

Never had my words seemed so insufficient.

I wanted to say the right thing but realized again that actions speak louder than words and that my being there would have to say what words lacked.

We hugged, rather I leaned down to kiss and hug her, and she muttered a greeting; giving me a little sideways smile. Her language was slurred, and Derek explained how he had been giving her the morphine as the nurse had directed him to. He showed me the locked box. I asked him if he felt tempted and he said no. He wanted to stay clean more than he wanted to use; he wanted to be with his mother. It had been hard for him the last few weeks watching her decline so rapidly, but he said that they were closer than ever.

Nanci was always positive and stayed upbeat, telling him that she was going to get tickets for a Red Sox game for his birthday coming up in July. He was a huge fan, but he had never been to Fenway to see a game. He followed all the games and told me how they always watched them together.

He felt good about being able to be there with Nanci now. He said there really wasn't anyone else who could have come.

Nanci's older daughter was not doing all that well herself; caught up in her own problems with addiction. It seems their relationship had been estranged for some time and he wasn't sure of what had really gone on between the two of them.

As I stood over the bed, a large wet stain appeared.

Poor baby, I thought. It's come to this.

I wanted to change the sheet and clean and dry her, but she didn't want me to. But I rolled her to her side and with Derek's help, got the wet sheet off the bed. I washed her with a washcloth and we put on a fresh sheet.

Where are the special soft scented cleansing cloths and the powder? There is nothing here to make this better for her, I thought to myself.

She wasn't thrilled with what was going on and let me know it. Her disease had not diminished her spirit and her love for her son wanted to spare him seeing any of this.

–Nanci, sweetheart, I can't leave you in a wet bed. I'm sorry, but I have to do this. I just want you to be more comfortable, I said to her.

Derek and I went in the kitchen and I told him what a good job he had done helping me and that his mom would be so proud of him. I gave him a hug and we stood there as sobs shook through his big body. No young man should have to see his mother like that.

I went back in to talk with her, sitting at the edge of the bed. I did most of the talking; she was weaker than even an hour ago. I told her what was in my heart about our shared history, our common struggle, and the miracle of our meeting. Her courage inspired me and our eyes locked. I said I wanted to cook a meal for Derek and asked her what his favorite food was.

She smiled, the first big one I'd seen since I'd gotten there and said, very clearly: –Steak.

Coming back from the store with steak and other ingredients, I started to cook a meal in her tiny kitchen. A small window opened from her bedroom to the kitchen and

I know she could hear us talking and cooking together, the smell of food filling the space.

Checking in on her frequently, giving her ginger ale to sip through a straw as her mouth was so dry. We began to eat, then stopped when her restlessness called for another dose of morphine.

After we ate, we looked through boxes of photos and Nanci finally fell into a deep sleep.

Derek was going through all the pictures, picking out ones he could make into a memory board. There would be a service soon and he wanted the best photos he could find. I saw her whole life through those photos and he told me the stories that went with them. I saw baby pictures of the man I now sat with. The hours were passing, and I wanted to get on the highway before dark. All too soon we were saying our goodbyes.

Her eyes stayed closed as I leaned in to put my face close to hers and say my last goodbye.

–Nanci, I love you and you will always be in my heart.

The tears came on the drive home; the sadness of a life ruined by addiction and now dying in poverty overwhelmed me.

I cried too for the love and devotion that I had seen in their home; this was the highest expression of love, caring for a dying person.

No truer amends could be made than what I had seen in that little trailer.

I cried too for Derek, as I watched him sort through those old pictures, looking for the ones that showed a smiling Nanci, in the good days, before the pain I know both of them had seen so much of.

He found the best happy picture of the two of them with

her arm thrown around his shoulder and a big open smile on her face.

It took me a long time to unwind when I got home; I kept replaying all I had heard and seen. I wasn't ready to let it go just yet. I slept heavily that night and called Derek as soon as I woke up.

I asked how the night had been for them. He asked me if Gary had called and I said no, why?

Nanci had died a few hours after I had left.

Goosebumps filled my body and I felt so grateful that I had driven up to see her.

Listening to my instincts, I somehow knew that time was running out.

Being with Nanci on her last day and being there to support and comfort Derek gave me a strong sense of meaning.

This is what it is all about. Helping each other. Being there for each other. Running towards what I used to run from. No longer afraid, I can feel everything. I am fully alive. I am full of gratitude.

*

The next day Ted came home from work—he had been given four tickets to a Red Sox game. The game was the weekend of Derek's birthday and Ted thought I should call and invite him to go with us.

We met Derek in Boston with his cousin and after lunch, we went to Fenway Park and found our way to the best seats Ted had ever been given.

Less than a week after her death, happiness found a way into Derek's life.

We collectively felt that Nanci was looking down on us, cheering and laughing that her wish for Derek to get to a Red Sox game had come true.

She had somehow gotten those tickets for him.

It was such a moment of synchronicity and a reckoning of how tragedy and joy can be two sides of the same coin.

33

Life is about saying yes to the mystery of the future, not about endless refinements of the past. –Tad Friend

What if my daughters don't want to meet me?

I spent many more therapy sessions with Brenda, playing out all the *what ifs*, leaving her office and taking the stairs to give myself a few extra minutes before I got in the car and back to real life.

Accept the things I cannot change. I have prayed to accept whatever the outcome is. I feel that coming as far as I have with this search is its own reward. It is tangible evidence that I've been willing to go through all the steps that bring me up to this moment. If they don't want to meet me, at least I can say to myself, you have done everything that you can do.

Also, I would remind myself that *no, not now* is not the same as *no, never.* I would hold onto the hope that everything would turn out as it should.

What if they hate me?

As certain as Lilli was that her life was over when Rob and I divorced, she will admit that her feelings have changed.

If Kim and Elle have been holding onto negative feelings all these years, it will take a miracle to change their hearts.

I hoped that my search for them would be that miracle,

but I could be wrong.

In many ways, it's probably good that I waited so many years. I had the relationships with my own children to nurture and care for. Caught up in my own losses, they also had been neglected and I needed to be there for them now. There were so many relationships that needed to be healed.

What if they are ill, incarcerated, dead or dying?

This is probably my worst fear, that it is too late. If they are alive and any of those other conditions exist, am I still willing to be present?

My tendency is to run from situations where I might be uncomfortable, situations where strong feelings are present.

Will I be able to handle it?

What if I couldn't control my feelings?

The fear of losing control was imminent, the fear I would drop into an abyss I couldn't climb out of.

When I first considered beginning a search, these initial anxieties felt like a conspiracy that kept me paralyzed.

*

As I walked further along a life that allowed me to pursue dreams that had been set aside, I returned to the study of art. At first a drawing class at the Jamestown Community Center, then oil painting at the Coleman Center, the educational branch of the Newport Art Museum, and then a college course at Massachusetts College of Art. I felt energized and the next semester I started attending classes at the Lyme Academy. I wasn't interested in a degree; I just wanted to learn the fundamentals from the best.

My first contact about my daughters came when I was settling into my car at the Lyme Academy, classes done for the day. It was a ninety-minute drive from Old Lyme, CT back to Newport, and I usually listened to books on tape to pass the time.

The call came from the social worker saying that she had non-identifying information about my daughters that she was now at liberty to share with me. As soon as that call ended, before I gave myself time to process the flood of emotions that I was feeling, I called a friend and told her about the conversation.

I am so grateful Leslie picked up the phone; my head was spinning with more questions, thoughts, and feelings. When I share those terrifying feelings, their hold on me seems to loosen its grip. Leslie, in her most gentle way, listened and I felt supported by her love and understanding.

What if they are needy, emotionally ill or psychologically damaged?

The question here is really: what if I feel they make demands on me that I cannot fulfill?

What if I feel that I am responsible for any of those conditions and now it's up to me to fix them?

I have done enough work on myself in recovery that I know that I'm not responsible for everyone else's feelings about themselves.

On the other hand, I told myself, how can a little child not be affected when their parents just walk out of their lives? There is a behavioral or psychological condition that results from the loss of one or both parents that is called the *abandoned child syndrome*—parents who leave their children, with or without good reason, can cause psychological damage to the child.

This is not recognized as a mental disorder, but I still had to reassure myself that all of us were adopted into homes where we were wanted and loved was expressed in a healthy way. Our parents had done the best they could with what they had.

I never gave much thought to the fact that I was given up for adoption at five days until Brenda and I did so much work surrounding those feelings.

Did I feel a separation from my birth mother as an infant?

Did that early abandonment affect all my relationships that were to follow?

Was that at the core of early alcohol and drug abuse?

Has my whole life's journey been about finding wholeness and self-acceptance?

When I look closer, I see how fear of abandonment has been a constant thread through my life; seeing it helps me to let go of its power.

What if I don't like what I find?

Liking or not liking was not a concern; I just wanted to know them as they are today. We are all imperfect and I wanted to let go of judgment and any preconceived ideas of how they would be.

You left them once, but after this search, if you find them, you cannot leave them again. Brenda was very definite about that.

I had never considered so many of the questions that came up in that room. When I try to think through things on my own, I reach the limitations of my own mind. Brenda guided me in a kind and loving way to look at so many possible scenarios.

Sometimes doing nothing *is* the best course of action.

It's a decision in its own right and can stand alone. Sometimes the way isn't clear and it's best to do nothing rather that some action that's half-baked just because you can't stand the feeling of doing nothing.

Doing nothing can be an overwhelming feeling for people like me, who like to feel they're in control, who like to feel they have answers.

Sometimes the answers aren't clear and there is a waiting period. Waiting to get more information so a better decision can be made; what we know as *an informed decision*. Not acting on impulse is a big change for me; to slow down and pause for a moment and let intuition speak its wisdom.

Sometimes there is nothing that can be done, and you find a way to accept whatever it is. Non-doing was a screen that stood in front of fear.

But now I had to come to a point where, intellectually, I was willing to go straight into the fear; if it devoured me, then so be it.

I had to get to the other side and as I had heard so many times, I would have to walk through my fear. All of my intellectual and emotional blocks were being heaved aside for a new courage that I did not recognize as my own.

It also helped to consider my motives at this point.

It gave me a reason, a purpose if you like, that was bigger than me. Since they had both gone to different families, they didn't even know they had a sister.

Of course, I hoped the end result would bring a reunion with my daughters, but I also thought of myself as a facilitator; who else could bring them to each other but me? I could easily unlock the mystery of their beginnings, and now finally, I would.

34

They always say time changes things, but you actually have to change them yourself. —Andy Warhol

—I gave up two children for adoption in 1968 and I would like to speak to someone about that.

I tried to keep all the emotion out of my voice. I didn't want them to think I was a nut case.

Why am I worried about what they think of me?

What the hell am I doing here, I thought to myself?

At the same time, I thought as I did before: if it ends here, at least I have taken the action that I can.

I had found the number for the Fairfax County Division of Child Services and had finally made the call.

Let go of the outcome.

Stay calm.

Breathe.

I was trying to stay in control. I didn't want to start blubbering on the phone; I wanted to sound like a woman who knew what she wanted and knew what steps to take to get her there.

I didn't want anyone to see the insides of me, the insecurity and panic that lived too close to the surface to disguise.

Evidently, I spoke in a cohesive way and they said the next step was to write a letter with my request. After a few flubbed starts to find a clear and honest voice I wrote the letter.

I am a birth mother in search of two children I surrendered for adoption in 1968 in Fairfax County, Virginia.

I was born in Portsmouth, NH and was adopted as an infant. I surrendered my daughters. Here I give their names and their birth dates. I was living in Fairfax, Virginia at this time, had been arrested for possession of marijuana and my children had been put in foster care. I was a teenage alcoholic, very sick and confused and decided the best thing to do was to sign the papers so that they could find permanent homes. I felt I was unable to care for them.

I believe they were adopted by two different families. They were born in Washington, DC, I was married to their father at the time. Here I give his name and birth date. We were divorced shortly thereafter.

In 1976, I got sober and haven't had a drink since. After a lengthy search, with full support from my adoptive family, I found my biological mother in 2006 when the laws for adoption records changed in my birth state of NH. I found out that my birth mother died of breast cancer, her sister and niece also had died of breast cancer. My biological mother was 45 years old when she died.

I wish for my daughters to be given this medical information. I wish for my daughters to learn of each other's existence, so that they may have a relationship with each other, if they so desire. I also wish to meet them, if they agree, so that I might speak with them about our lives, past and present. Thank you for all your efforts to help me.

This is at the essence of my request, to allow me to connect the circle from which my life began and open a door which was once closed and bring lives and hearts together. This is my hope. I believe that this process is the right thing to do and pray that you grant my request.

I sent the letter off and began the wait.

35

The world breaks everyone, and afterward, some are strong at the broken places. –Ernest Hemingway

Somewhere along the way, my therapy sessions turned to my relationship with my mother. I knew it would eventually surface, but I wasn't looking forward to going back there. I didn't want to feel all the painful times; the longing I had when I heard other women talk about how close they were to their mothers. It hadn't been that way for so much of my life.

You might say that I'm a slow learner.

Today I can only deal or learn things when the timing is right and the first requirement for me is a sense of being open to the outcome. I can't learn, and I can't grow if I am always so caught up in what I think the outcome should be.

I was never the kind of person who would be able to let go and trust but that's who I had to become to do this work.

So much of my past behavior has been based on motives that were self-seeking. I would do something that looked like it was good, but underneath the motive wasn't so good.

I don't want to be the woman who waited until it was too late. I don't want to be the woman who has regrets; not with the knowledge that I have about myself today.

There is no easy way out of this even now; one sentence

follows another, and memories come to me in dreams.

*

My mother's drinking had escalated as the years had gone by and I think she resented me a little for getting sober.

It wasn't because she wasn't glad that I was getting to a better place with my life but because she thought I was now judging her.

To be perfectly honest, though, I *was* judging her.

Sometimes, I had to walk on eggshells around her. I would try to gauge her mood. If I thought she'd take anything I might say personally, I would steer the subject in another direction.

When she had too much to drink, she would get down on herself. What had she done with her life that was remarkable? I tried to feel sympathy for her, but I only felt the differences between us. It was suggested that I read and do the exercises in a book subtitled: *Women and Food Obsession* which had a large section on mother-daughter relationships.

Fat and Furious by Judi Hollis.

Oh, how I hated the title of that book, but oh, how much I learned about the relationship with my mother from working with it.

Exercise—Telling Mom what she missed.

Dear Mummy, You missed out on helping me to know myself when I was so confused and afraid when we moved to France. You were so caught up in being the perfect Navy wife; it felt like that was your full-time job. You couldn't get through my façade and missed being able to help me navigate the changes. You missed being there innumerable times, because of your drinking, you missed your grandchildren. They are so incredible, but you never got close enough to know them. We could have gone to the beach, the museum, the zoo, and so many places together. I wish you had been there.

You missed out on being your own woman; you were so dependent on Daddy for everything. You missed out on claiming your own power; instead you compared yourself to others and came up short. You let yourself be intimidated by others who you thought were judging you.

Exercise—Telling Mom how she was hurt.

I know today it must have hurt you deeply when my first marriage ended and your granddaughters were taken out of your life. We never talked about it, but I know that's when you starting to drink more to numb the pain. I was so self-centered I didn't even see how much my choices hurt you. I never looked at things through your eyes.

Exercise—Thanking Mom.

Dear Mummy, Thank you for all the things you did give me, a love of books and reading, art, theater and the whole world of culture and civilization and a great appreciation of it. You had such a challenge with me; the baby you had waited so long for grew up to be a nightmare of worry and fear. When I got kicked out of Concord for smoking, when I ran away one summer, when I flunked algebra and then geometry and then when I got pregnant. One thing after another. I wish I'd been able to think through some of my impulsive behavior and see the consequences—the disappointment and pain I caused you and Daddy. I wish I hadn't been so blind to everything outside my own little world.

I could have added more to that exercise.

I could have thanked her for wanting me, adopting me, and calling me special. She always stood by me, never wanted me out of her life. She never shamed me or called me names.

She loved Daddy with her whole heart and showed me

how much she enjoyed their relationship.

She accepted my friends and my boyfriends and wasn't judgmental of them. She knew how to mind her own business and didn't pry into my life. She wanted to be more than she was—a better cook, grandmother, a smarter and more educated person, a more loving person.

Sometimes she complained and whined that no one needed her, wanted her or loved her. I don't remember how I handled those times, but I do remember Daddy ignoring her. He knew it was the alcohol talking, he knew too that no words could fill the emptiness she felt.

I have felt that emptiness too.

In recovery, when I am vulnerable, I can break down the barriers and let others in. I learn who to trust, who is safe. I am being shaped to live a life of interdependence, finding a healthy balance in my relationships with others.

I had so many more opportunities with my life that she did. I have a partner who is able to talk about feelings, who understands the language of the heart. I have models of women who inspire me by being true to themselves, not just standing beside a man and thinking that should bring self-fulfillment. I am living in an era where women empower each other while seeking balance in their lives.

And even still, she was so much more than I ever gave her credit for.

She had a much greater impact on me than I had considered before.

She was doing the best she could, feeling like me that life was overwhelming at times and alcohol gave her, for a brief moment, a way to relax. I knew she was an only child, often more a companion to her parents than a little girl trying to figure out who she was. She lived in China when she was only four and moved around with a military family just as I had. I remember hearing of her natural athleticism, her guts in the game of field hockey, her speed and grace figure skating.

She had a library of spiritual books, C.S. Lewis and all he had written, hoping to find an answer to ease her spiritual unrest. She had an insatiable thirst for knowledge. Her life as a naval officer's wife was a challenge, her job was to complement him and keep the focus on him. She had to let go of personal ambition in favor of supporting his ambition. Her life was second to his.

She felt raising children was hard and sometimes she felt overwhelmed, but she didn't want anyone to know that. She wanted everyone to think she was doing fine.

She suffered by comparing herself to others and coming up short. Me too.

She didn't think she was pretty enough, smart enough, or just enough. Me too.

She felt less than, and intimidated by, people she thought might judge her. Me too.

I eventually saw her more like me than not and found compassion and peace in that.

She loved me unconditionally, appreciating me, and letting me know she was proud of me.

She gave me her *blessings* to find my birth mother. She let go of me.

She stayed connected with people to the end and when that end came, she was surrounded by loved ones. Her greatest strengths came in adversity—when Daddy died, there was no self-pity or complaining.

She was always brave and never gave up.

She did her very best.

Our struggles are a piece of who I am—I could not be me without her.

36

Do the thing you fear and the death of fear is certain.
                                    –Ralph Waldo Emerson

I compose a letter to the parents.

I find a time when I won't be disturbed, as I want to get a first draft written. I'm feeling a little anxious. I want to sound like a sincere and good person. I am looking for a positive response from them.

It's a neutral sounding letter, not descriptive of what really happened in my life, but a synopsis that I hope will appeal to them enough so that I might be able to contact my daughters.

It seems outrageous that women in their forties are being protected by this law, but there appears to be no time limit to the restrictions. I am willing to do whatever it takes. I've been told the next step is for me to write to the parents, and they may or may not give permission that their daughters can be contacted by me. It all happens through Norah, the caseworker assigned to help.

Dear Parents

When you adopted my daughter over forty years ago you saved our lives in so many ways. I was adopted myself as an infant and I often heard how my parents had wanted a child of their own for so long. They were married for ten years before they finally adopted me. My sister was born two years later and I grew up knowing I had been adopted. I have learned firsthand how important reconnecting the birth ties can be after finding my own birth family several years ago. I don't know how long you had waited for a child, but I thank you from the bottom of my heart.

Having since raised four children now, 31, 29-year-old twins and an 18-year-old, I know the challenges that parenting can bring. It can strain the best relationship and break your heart when your child makes poor decisions. It can also fill you with such love and pride as they grow and you witness that growth through the years. Raising a child is the hardest job in the world and I know the sacrifices you must have made when you adopted my daughter. It takes so much strength and maturity to be a good parent and I thank you for opening your hearts and your lives to her.

My children have taught me many lessons about real love, patience, self-sacrifice and acceptance. These are all qualities I lacked when I found out I was pregnant at age 16. I insisted on keeping my baby and the father and I got married. We were kids having kids and when I found out I was pregnant for the second time when my daughter was less than three months old, the marriage started to crumble. We didn't have the maturity to handle our lives and I became very depressed. I know today that I had a severe case of post-partum depression, but I didn't know it then. I did know that something was dreadfully wrong with me, because I was so full of fear and felt a sense of impending doom. I thought I should have all the answers as to how to be a parent, but we were in way over our heads. We were both so emotionally immature and ill-equipped to handle a family and to be good parents. We made a desperate decision to give up the girls. I prayed that they would find homes with good people who could care for them better than we could. The marriage ended at the same time. I felt I had failed at motherhood. I thank you for loving her and keeping her safe when I could not.

My hope today is that an exchange can begin between us. I respect the relationship you have with her and wish in no way to interfere with that. I would like to give you the opportunity to ask any questions that you might have. I would like to know about my daughter and I would like for her to know about me. I would like for her to know that she has a sister. The woman I am today at almost sixty is worlds away from the confused teenager I was when giving birth so many years ago. I am a grandmother now and feel the wondrous and special joy of those miraculous new lives. I know today that I am a positive and enriching presence in my children and grandchildren's lives.

Dear Parents, we are connected by our history and by our choices—mine to let go and yours to receive. I do not wish to disrupt your lives in any negative way. I pray for an opportunity to complete the circle of my life and of theirs. I pray that we may begin a journey of sharing our stories with each other.

I hope to hear from you.
07/09/2008

I am at their mercy while I wait. I have made copies of the letter, so they each receive the same letter. My desire is that my daughters learn they each have a sister; I want them to know that much and I'm the only one who has that information. I am the only one with so much of the information and I'm constantly wishing that it was clearer to me, that there weren't so many gaps. First the letters have to go to Norah, the case worker, then they have to be screened to ensure there is no identifiable information in them, and then the letters will be sent to the parents, who hold my fate in their hands.

I worry that I haven't sounded sincere enough.

I worry that they will dismiss me without giving me a chance; that the whole thing will just die with the letters.

I worry they will be tossed in the trash along with the weekly circulars advertising Virginia hams and ten lemons for two dollars.

I wait and worry that they will say yes, you sound like someone we want to meet, and we are all onboard.

What will happen then?

The thoughts swirl through my mind.

I read the *Rules for Reunion* the case worker has sent me and ponder each one.

Birthmothers may not "back off", especially if they searched.

Adoptees may express anger in some way, probably not overtly, possibly not even recognizing that he/she is angry.

Remember that real life is "messy."

The list filled a page and I wondered how many would apply to me.

37

We must let go of the life we have planned, so as to accept the one that is waiting for us. –Joseph Campbell

I'm told by my caseworker there was a mix up in the mail. Something was sent to the wrong address and that caused a delay.

I had thought the worst of course—that my letter had been read and rejected and the doorway to my hopes would be closed.

I prepared myself for the news by repeatedly saying to myself: —Everything happens for a reason. I will accept things as they are, not as I wish them to be.

But then, I received a letter with a form I needed to fill out and have notarized, so that I could exchange letters or pictures with the adoptive families. It would allow the agency to act as an intermediary for the purpose of exchanging non-identifying information and pictures.

I finally received a phone call from Norah who said both sets of parents had agreed, and she gave me my daughters' phone numbers. I wrote the numbers down in awe and disbelief. She gave me a brief history, things that they had shared with her that she now had permission to share with me.

She would be calling them next and doing the same thing. It seemed completely surreal to me; that after so many years, they were so completely within my reach by phone.

I called Kim first and when she didn't pick up, I left a message. When she returned my call, I had just pulled into my driveway and I sat in the car to talk with her.

Kim had the most basic of questions: Why did you give me up?

My body started to shake involuntarily as I took us back in time and memories.

She said that she had tried to search for me for years and had exhausted every avenue. She came up with nothing.

She said that she loved to read and had kept journals for as long as she could remember. I said that I couldn't imagine life without books and that I journaled too.

She said she had trouble with alcohol and drugs when she was younger, and I said, me too.

She said that she had three children and her middle was a son she had named Seth.

I told her I had three too, and my middle child was a son that I had named...Seth.

He was named after my grandfather, a solid and old-fashioned name that brought back beautiful memories of my special relationship with him. One coincidence after another was shared as Kim and I talked about our lives and the paths we had walked.

She said she had a picture of herself on an Oriental rug and asked me about it. It was navy and lighter blue patterns on a buff colored background and had been in the living room of my parents' apartment in Washington. We would return occasionally to visit and had taken Kim's picture as she was beginning to crawl.

Hearing her describe the only photo she had was very emotional—I remember when I had also given up all my photos. The social worker way back then had advised this, that it would help me in the *moving on* process.

Why hadn't I kept them anyway?

I wanted it all behind me honestly. I had no idea how impossible that would be.

Events from our past are never forgotten, the details of the memories may fade while other memories are forever vivid; it's only how we feel and think about those memories that can change. More healing will come about if a person can view the events through different eyes. I had to look upon my past with compassion instead of regret and judgement.

Why could I treat everyone else with more love and understanding than I could ever give myself?

Today, when I sense I'm headed toward negativity in my thinking, I stop myself. I may not be responsible for that first thought, but where the second thought leads me, I do have some control over. I can turn my thinking in a different direction; usually to gratitude and all the blessings in my life. Stopping for a breath can be a starting point too, of changing the old thought patterns. At times, this is a great effort; other times it flows easily. It's progress not perfection. I remind myself that I am human first.

Kim and I talked for a very long time. At times we cried, at times there was silence as I searched my heart for the most honest answer to her questions. We connected.

*

My baby girl was adopted quickly and she was renamed Elle. It was a miracle that I connected with her at all.

The letter had somehow been sent to her father, even

though her parents had been divorced for quite some time. He contacted her which might not have happened if the letter had gone to her mother. Her mother was just being protective and cautious, wondering what I would want with Elle now.

Again, the talk was long and sweet, and we shared deeply with each other about our lives. Again, the similarities were startling; we had both taught yoga and loved to write. Journaling had been a refuge for us when emotions overwhelmed. We got to know ourselves through our own words. She sounded like a very old soul to me; so gentle and wise. I answered all her hard questions the best that I could. The joy of talking with her overrode the pain I felt when going together so far back in time. I wished I had more clarity to give.

38

There are only two ways to live your life. One is as though nothing is a miracle. The other is as though everything is a miracle.

—Albert Einstein

I decided that I would meet Kim first since she was my firstborn. I was trying to be logical.

I couldn't decide how long the trip should be though; too short and we would barely say hello before it was time to say goodbye. It might seem that I didn't want to invest any time with her and I didn't want her to feel like that.

If the visit was too long, I was afraid it would put pressure on both of us. Maybe we would run out of things to say and we would be left staring at each other.

I had all kinds of crazy thoughts going through my head before I finally made a decision.

I booked a flight to San Diego and a hotel hoping it wouldn't be too far from where she lived.

I tried to take a breath, but I was anxious inside.

I thought of all the reasons I had not to do the search to begin with and then, with great gratitude, thought of how far I had really come.

So many fears that had kept me in the dark about my daughters for so long had been faced and I had come through them all.

I had to trust that everything would work out providing I

kept my heart open and let go of any expectations. So, it was that on a sunny California afternoon I found myself, suitcase in tow, on the pavement outside the terminal in San Diego, waiting for Kim.

I had called when I landed and now I was in the designated spot.

She came towards me with a big smile and pace quickening, arms opening, we were hugging each other tightly as though we were the only people there.

She was tiny and slim, decorated with tattoos and jewelry, her brown eyes made up with smoky shadow and liner emphasizing their size.

Her hair was long and hung in loose waves. An embroidered shoulder bag hung by her hip. A long halter dress with a flowered print reminded me of how I had dressed at nineteen; the dimple in her chin the same as mine too.

I pushed incredulity aside and couldn't get the smile off my face. I was actually here! Standing with my daughter. It was nothing short of a miracle. Even if you don't believe in miracles, this meeting was beyond what I ever could have hoped for.

We went to her car then to her house and she started to make dinner and introduced me to her daughters, Chelsea and Jophie.

Her son wasn't home but had promised her that he would be there for dinner. She showed me around, all the girls had their own rooms and Seth had taken over the garage that was attached to the house and made it a boy cave.

I felt right at home with all the books, art and encompassing bohemian vibe.

She had a dog, a cat, a fish tank and a big backyard full of exotic tropical plants. She had a palm tree and an orange tree they could pick fruit from.

She loved color and I settled into the cushiony sofa after dinner, feeling comfortable. She had made a vegetarian pasta dish and Seth had made it home in time for us to eat together. She said they were mostly vegetarian; her shoes were made of pleather.

They sang a grace she had taught them when they were children and I saw and felt how close the four of them were. I felt welcomed and at home and I thought how so often what I worry about never comes to pass anyway.

Later that night, back at the hotel, it had taken quite a while to fall asleep, my mind and heart were too full to not let the feelings linger.

The next day we went to the zoo, just the two of us. A perfectly blue sky and we looked around together and talked and just enjoyed a day of being close, gazing at animals and slowly walking the pathways.

Her children met us by the pier and we went to dinner, one big happy family.

I looked around the table and really felt overwhelmed that this was actually happening; for so long I hadn't allowed myself to even think about anything like this.

I didn't think I was worthy of meeting her or even of finding her.

When you don't think you deserve anything, you accept less and less of the bounty life holds for you.

We had been at Kim's house and getting ready to go out to dinner when Chelsea decided she needed to color her hair. She couldn't wait to do it later, it had to be done right then. I stepped into the tiny bathroom, standing above her while she sat on the toilet, I applied the product to her long hair.

—I've done this before, but never on hair as long as yours.

—Don't worry it will be fine.

So we got to know each other in the bathroom, in a setting I couldn't have dreamed up on my own. When I'm open, anything can happen. I can have a moment with a granddaughter that I only met the day before and feel a bond between us. My granddaughter! I get shivers when I think about how this trip has brought such peace and wonder to our lives. Here is the flesh and blood of us, still here and still wanting a love together.

The time flew by while we did ordinary things and then we were standing outside my hotel saying goodbye.

The last night we lingered in deep cushioned chairs before a huge fire pit at my hotel. The air had a chill to it, but we couldn't stop talking. We started to shiver and kept on talking. We didn't want the night to end.

She was a night owl and I remember being that way too. The late nights had thrown me off my natural rhythms, but I didn't care.

Saying goodbye took a long time for both of us; standing by her car hugging, talking, and then hugging again. Neither one of us wanted to let go. It was painful but in the good way of really feeling what was happening in the moment, neither one of us was anywhere but right there where time stopped for us.

My flight home was early the next morning and I slept exhausted across the country.

39

Where there is great love, there are always miracles. –Willa Cather

It was much easier logistically to see Elle, since she was on the East Coast, not too far from Washington, DC.

I had several conversations with her about meeting up as well as talks with my cousin, Mary, who lived in DC.

One talk with Elle was about the healing power of art. She told me how she used to think she had found healing through writing and we envisioned how we could merge our writing with artmaking.

We spoke of the Tibetan mandalas, intricately made of colored sand, made as a prayer, and then swept away. Sending the prayer into the world. Impermanence. Non-attachment.

I drove down about a month after meeting Kim, arriving in DC at Mary's house, a sweet brick townhouse. I had hit the Washington rush hour and I was happy to finally get out and park the car.

She had sold the big house that we had previously visited after her divorce, but she had stayed in the neighborhood where she had been for forty years. She was so welcoming, this cousin I didn't really know, who had seemed so distant when I went to Concord Academy so long ago. She had been totally supportive about my search. We went to a local restaurant and walking over there I could understand what she loved about her neighborhood: the shops, pubs, and brownstones held a comfortable and safe feeling, away from the clamor of downtown. We ate dinner, and I planned for the next day. Before heading back to her house, we went by the subway station for a preview dry run.

Scenarios of meeting Elle played through my head and I wrestled with fatigue until I finally dozed off in the downstairs guest room. The smell of bacon and coffee woke me up even though I hadn't heard Mary bustling about in the kitchen.

She fed me an egg sandwich and I left to catch my train—the orange line to Vienna. I finally got to the last stop, slightly disoriented turning right not left, then correcting myself and going with the flow of people to the stairs.

At the top of the stairs a woman and I walked by each other, then instantly doubled back with innate intuition. Moments later we were hugging and kissing, holding nothing back. Her long hair was streaked with blonde and she was small and so like Kim I was startled. Her face was without makeup and her body simply clothed, unadorned by jewelry. She is a natural woman, I thought at once. We laughed, then hugged, then walked to her car.

—Do you mind if I smoke?

—Of course not, I said.

She gave me a tour of the area and eventually down to her childhood home.

We were parked catty corner to the house when we spotted a man heading to his mailbox. Elle leaped out of the car to talk with him and then beckoned me to follow as he had invited us into the house.

He gave us a tour room by room and she told me how everything had been when she lived there.

She showed me the room where her mother retreated to sew, the mantle where the row of family pictures stood, and the window that was above her bed in her little room. I could imagine her running through the house and thought sadly of all I had missed of her life. We walked outside to a sunny corner of the property where her mom had a big kitchen garden and Elle's love of gardening began.

We sat a bit in the yard and she shared more memories; then we had our picture taken by the homeowner. We are sitting very close our bodies touching on her old front steps.

*

A short drive brought us to Great Falls Park where we climbed giant boulders to get close to the waterfall and she shared how much being in nature was a part of who she was.

Sitting together on a huge slab of rock, she pulled out a small tape recorder and asked if I could tell her son a story of how I was at his age. She held the microphone up to my lips and I spoke about being in school in France. She said she had to look all over to find the little recording device; how quickly things become obsolete. In that moment by the thundering falls we felt the chasm of the lost years between us. We stayed quiet for a little while, each of us lost in thought.

We found someone to take our picture before leaving; leaning against the guardrail with our arms around each other, we smiled. Posed on a rock, long windblown hair, she squinted with sun in her eyes for yet one more picture to engrave her face in my mind.

Later at a Thai restaurant, we ordered dishes we didn't finish; pushing aside the plates so we could better hear and see each other. The hours together were coming to an end, she drove me back to the train station and we hugged one more time.

Practically out of body surreal, yet completely real, I thought to myself. The briefness of our meeting had somehow made it more intense. As I waited for the train, and on the ride back into the city, I played back every moment of our time over and over in an endless loop. I let my eyes close and I saw her face.

When I reached Mary's house, I fell into her arms, feeling so emotional, happy and drained at the same time.

—I know what will be good for you, she said.

She drew me a hot tub and filled it with lavender salts and I sunk back into the water and let myself feel her mothering love. We didn't talk until later and she sat and listened, knowing what a part she had played in my first reunion with Elle.

*

Driving back to Rhode Island the next day I thought about how much had happened in the last month. The towns went by me in a blur as I replayed the miracles that had come to pass. What if I had never started the search? Kim had told me that she had been searching for me since she was fifteen and had given up hope of ever finding me. Elle had settled into a dull acceptance of her foggy past. And now everything had changed.

40

Life is stranger than any of us expected, there is a somber, imponderable fate. Enigma rules and the heart has no certainty.
                                                        —Richard Eberhart

Huffing is a type of substance abuse that involves inhaling fumes from household substances in order to experience a high. Also known as sniffing or inhalant abuse, this practice is undertaken to feel euphoria or hallucinations; however, it is an extremely risky form of substance abuse. —American Addiction Centers

Kim and Elle wanted to find out more about their birth father. I gave them all the information I had. Their search initially took them down blind alleys and finally dead-ended at the truth.

Billy took off after our marriage ended. The summer of love had passed but it wasn't too late to go to California to see what was going on.

There was still a huge influx of hippies and he was among them. He met a kid named Sammy and got a job at the Ojai Orange packing house somewhere along the Maricopa Highway in Ventura County.

A friend from work said he could stay with him; he lived with his mother not far from their job. She found an aerosol paint can with the bottom split, wrapped in cloth—they had been sniffing the saturated material.

The boys took off, with the intention of hitchhiking to Texas.

They had been on the road a couple of days when Billy was picked up by the Highway Patrol. They had observed him vomiting uncontrollably and had called an ambulance.

He told the doctors he had been vomiting for two days. They treated him and released him less than four hours later and the boys went back to where they had been staying.

Five days later Billy was brought back to hospital and admitted he had used multiple drugs, LSD, and had been sniffing paint thinner for three days. There was dried blood on his lips.

The following day he had a grand-mal seizure. The day after that he had a second seizure and failed to improve or respond to treatment. He died on an October day in 1969. He was twenty-two years old.

His father received the coroner's report back home in Virginia two days before Christmas:

CAUSE OF DEATH: Accident/inhalation of volatile hydrocarbons causing acute hemorrhagic pulmonary edema.

I had never thought of him dying so young, or so very long ago.

I just presumed he would go on and on, like I had done. Maybe the girls search would find him in recovery or dead of heart failure in his fifties.

Maybe he was fat and happy and had moved to Arizona. There was no way any of us thought we would learn he had died at twenty-two, an agonizing end to the search for happiness.

He had found his escape and I felt so sad; he was just a kid for god's sake.

The California dream had ended for him in a nightmare.

Now everyone had their answers, but it gave no satisfaction.

Again, I grieved a man I had once loved.

41

Breathe it all in, love it all out. —Mary Oliver

A year passed since I had met both Elle and Kim, but they were getting no closer to meeting each other.

Financial restraints and complications of daily life seemed to always get in the way. Phone conversations connected them.

I felt a sense of responsibility to reunite them. It had been one of my primary reasons for finding them in the first place; so that they could each know they had a sister. I wanted them to be together.

I came up with a plan to have Kim fly to Baltimore, to have Elle drive up from her home, and I would drive down from Rhode Island and we would have a weekend reunion.

Everyone agreed, so I made the arrangements.

Elle got to the hotel an hour or so after I arrived. When she knocked on the door, my breath caught, I sent up a prayer of thanks and opened the door. It was special to spend some time with her alone before Kim joined us. We shared anticipation and talked like the long-lost souls that we were. My heart was so full that they would soon be meeting each other again.

When we picked Kim up from the airport, the initial hugs of greeting over, they walked closely together, shoulders touching, sliding together into the back seat of my car, as they would have done if only months had passed instead of decades. Sisters. Listening to their soft voices as they searched for memories from each other, for a common thread to their story, I felt a deep sense of accomplishment as I drove back to the hotel.

I had done something right.

We hung the *Do Not Disturb* sign on the door of our suite and Elle led us through a yoga practice. She taught us chants and breathing and we let her be our teacher. In the darkened room, we moved beyond time and schedules and places to go and were directed only by her words.

We breathed full and deep and felt alive together as our breath blended and time became only the present moment.

Elle brought cookies laced with pot which Kim and I declined. I would eat a cookie too, if I could, but I don't take mind altering substances anymore. I'm feeling so grateful to be aware of everything going on without the haze. I'm alive with the clarity of the moment.

Kim says she will ask her recovery coach about pot for chronic pain when she gets back to California.

I let it go and thankfully don't become obsessed with Elle's cookie stash.

There's something though about the invitation that's so appealing to me, let's get high together. It's a way of connecting us quickly and without fanfare or effort.

The next morning, we drove to the graveyard where Sean was buried and Kim spent a long while by his grave. Her first true love, her soulmate; he died so young. He still lives for her, her pain no less with passing years, a tragedy she carries like a whisper. She has his name tattooed around her wrist in large cursive script, the letters forming a delicate bracelet around her wrist. I walk apart from them; I want to give them space. I want to take in the feeling of watching them walk along this cemetery path on this cold fall day. Stepping out of the center of this unfolding drama to witness my two girls walking, cigarettes dangling from their hands, seemed almost otherworldly to me.

We are together, and it feels so right. We saw the sights as tourists might, walked miles, talked hours, ate together and then the weekend was nearly over.

Our last night at the hotel, I shared my art journals and they passed them back and forth making comments that connected us all as artists—lovers of beauty and words.

Kim got her laptop out and began to share her poems, some so dark and painful to hear.

She is a fierce and intense writer.

I fell asleep from sheer exhaustion to their quiet voices deep in conversation. *I'm sleeping in the same room as my daughters.* I never allowed myself to think any of this could be possible. And yet, here we were.

In a few hours, I would have almost four hundred miles to drive and reflect upon our time together. It had been a transcendental experience and I remembered how we had stood side by side in front of the hotel's full-length mirror comparing heights, then eyes, noses, mouths, dimples.

We looked hard at our images and found the similarities we knew would be there. We grinned in unison.

When I woke the next morning, I studied their sleeping forms, Kim in the double bed next to mine, Elle on the sofa bed in the sitting room area.

The light was beginning to stream in and show the unremoved makeup around Kim's eyes, the bedclothes tangled and Elle's more restful form, buried beneath the blankets.

It hurt to know that early abandonment marked them forever. I will never forget my part in that, but today there is a new hope. Timing and grace united to give us all another chance.

We are so very much alike, our weaknesses and our strengths. We are all survivors of broken hearts and dreams and yet we dream on.

The stakes were high, but I trust that I've done my homework, that I've come prepared, that I have lowered my expectations as far as outcome is concerned and that love has been the motivating force throughout. I've put my faith in the healing power of love.

I planned to leave early, wanting to get on the road for the drive back home. I moved quietly in the bathroom, a quick shower, pulling on jeans then getting my bags together and taking them out to the car, so there would be nothing left to do but say goodbye before I left.

It never felt like I could do enough to be forgiven and as I prepared to leave, I sat down on the edge of Elle's bed and we talked for a while. Tears came with the flood of feelings I was having about leaving them again. She hugged me and said everything was okay and I felt comforted by her words. Kim was still groggy with sleep for our goodbyes and as I left the room quietly, Elle said to me:

–We don't have to say goodbye, we can say, *See you later.*

EPILOGUE

All manner of good things begin to flow in your direction once you begin to take action. –Jack Canfield

There were so many years of darkness around this whole subject. It was my shameful secret and I thought I would carry that shame for the rest of my life. Forgiveness was out of the realm of the possible.

I didn't know that in taking action the forgiveness that I had been praying for would be given. I didn't foresee how my experience could help someone else.

I wanted, above all else, to make it right.

It was really grace that opened the door and gave me enough courage to start taking steps.

With each step, I faltered; don't think for a minute that I wasn't filled with fear at what this undertaking really meant.

But by taking it one step at a time, I was able to do the impossible, then let go, breathe, and see what would or would not happen next.

I kept moving forward.

I didn't have to run away from my feelings. I found courage I had never thought myself capable of.

Looking at a banner with the words: *But for the grace of God* I feel an immense gratitude for my life today.

To greet a sunrise with delight instead of dread for an upcoming day is something I don't take for granted.

I have lost two husbands to the disease of addiction, both young and senseless deaths.

I never take it lightly, and as I see people coming in and out of recovery, thinking they will always get another chance for another shot at life, my heart aches.

I know that another chance doesn't always happen. It doesn't matter who you are, your economic or social standing can't protect you. Your brilliant mind can't protect you. If you are an addict and you continue to use, the chances aren't good.

Sobriety is a gift and you can't keep it unless you give it away. Not an original thought for me, as is so much of the wisdom and commonsense advice I've heard from others who have gone before me.

I listen with empathy and true connection with a heart that has simultaneously been transformed and healed. I have a sense of this is how it's supposed to be between people. All people.

On a phone call with my cousin who spends the winter in Florida, he was expressing his sympathy for the tough winter that New Englanders experience each year.

I replied that because we have a dog, we walk no matter what the weather is. We can't just wait for a sunny day, or a warm day, or a day without wind to walk Cooper.

So, it may be cold, windy and grey. It may be freezing, wind cutting my face and sleeting. It may be ugly, and I may have to dig deep to pile on the layers and get outside.

When I do, I may be rewarded with some tiny thing of beauty, some sliver of hope on the horizon, the colors igniting my spirit. It may just be a flash of light, the way a reflection looks, or the smell of the air and suddenly I am feeling grateful for all of it. My joy comes from a place inside of me; it's no longer dependent on outside circumstances.

My daughters thank me for finding them.

I still feel awe that my path had brought me so far.

I showed up and I did the work.

I set aside my fears and told the voices to back off.

I had to shut those voices up more than once as they conspired to keep me down and forever in regret.

All I ever wanted was to find Kim and Elle and that has happened.

All I ever wanted was for them to find each other and that has happened.

All I ever wanted was their forgiveness and some understanding of what happened, and that too has happened.

At one time, I just wanted a happy life that held no pain.

Today I can be grateful for the pain and know in my heart that no matter how far down I've been, someone can be touched and helped by my experience.

To say that I've gone through it all is trite and untrue for I do not know what is yet to come.

But I do know this.

I am not alone and because of that, I am no longer afraid.

ACKNOWLEGEMENTS

All shall be well, and all shall be well and all manner of thing shall be well. —Julian of Norwich

This journey has been long, at times painful, and at times joyful. It has never been without hope.

There are many I hold in my heart and wish to thank here.

My two mothers—Marilyn for giving me life and Ray for raising me with a questioning mind, an eye for beauty and a heart open to life.

My father for showing me true acceptance, a non-judgmental attitude and unconditional love. You are my hero.

My sister Marjorie for her uncanny ability to remember our childhood and her high regard for the abilities I so often question. Our similarities are far greater than our differences and though tragedies brought us close as adults, true sister love keeps us close today.

For all the men and women who taught me by their example to find my voice, get honest and tell my story. For showing me that I am not alone and that I never have to feel the way I once did- I owe you my life. For the women who opened their hearts to me, I am humbled by your trust.

A loving God who gave me the courage to change what I could—the way that I think about my past—so that I might share my experience and help others.

My children—Jessica, Seth and Lilli, I love you with my whole heart. You have encouraged me on this journey with your love, trust and support as I went back into my past. You are my second chance at motherhood. You are my teachers.

Jessica, your sensitivity is your greatest strength and your devotion to those you love inspires me. The shy child has transformed to a woman of great strength and purpose. You are my truth.

Seth, your wide-eyed enthusiasm, your deep well of creativity and sense of adventure have always been with you. You live life to the fullest and have stayed curious about everything and everyone. You are my vision seeker.

Lilli, you are the parent I aspire to be. You are an advocate, taskmaster, dream-reacher and always have put your children first. Your determination makes nothing impossible. You are my example.

The fathers of my children—the poetry we made together lives in the DNA of these five, bringing music and meaning to the love we once shared.

Ted, my husband—for your all-encompassing love and support in all the endeavors, tangents and interests, and my sometimes distracted way of approaching life. You are my rock and have encouraged this project all along. Your words—Never give up—sustain and motivate me each day. By your side, life is good.

Alex—my son by marriage, you gave me yet another chance to be a mom. Your courage and easy-going strength are deeply a part of who you are. Stay close to those who love you and never lose sight of who you are and the joy of living one day at a time.

Brenda Bachman MSW—for your loving encouragement and patience as I came to terms with my past and felt my way through the emotions of my complex life. I couldn't have gone to some of those dark places without you as my guide.

You promised me that I could get through it all to the light.

William Armitage—my editor, who appeared in my life at the right moment, to give order to my words, aligning events to give rhythm to my story and make what had been only a dream come to print. The synchronicity of it all! Thank you for your understanding, your wisdom and experience and your ever-calm demeanor to show and guide me through the process.

And finally, although nothing is ever final—my daughters Kim and Elle. Gratitude fills me each day that I found you and that you have allowed me to be part of your lives. Your forgiveness soothes my humble heart and I rise each day feeling joy for the grace and love of the universe.

ABOUT THE AUTHOR

Anne Winthrop Cordin lives with her husband, Ted, and their dog, Cooper, in Rhode Island and in their motorhome exploring the US.

She is an award-winning artist whose work can be seen at: annewinthropcordin.com *and* annewinthropcordinapainterspath.blogspot.com

You can also follow Anne's journeys and work on Instagram at: anne_winthrop_cordin

Made in the USA
Middletown, DE
20 December 2018